UNDER TH[

KYLE KEYES

UNDER THE BUS

KYLE KEYES

UNDER THE BUS

kylekeyes.com

KYLE KEYES

UNDER THE BUS

PRELUDE

Homicide detectives, Donde Clark and Juanito Lewis moved to Hobbs Creek just days before banker, Richard Ghetti was gunned down in the front room of his Lake Powhattan, water front cabin.

Barbershop talk had it that divine providence played some part in transferring the two NYC lawmen from the Big Apple to this backwater town in South Jersey. Hobbs Creek Police Chief, Alvin Phillips believed it was his lucky silver dollar. The Six-O-Clock news refused comment because the incident did not relate to the Corona virus.

Truth be, Donde's wife was mugged on three separate occasions outside a Brooklyn super market. After which, the outraged Donde sold their city row home, and the two urbanites headed for the country. Juanito came along because where there's a Clark, there's a Lewis.

    Both men had attended a NYC police academy, where they studied police procedure, weaponry, defensive driving, first aid, etc. etc. At that point in time, due to female applicants, the city had replaced height and weight requirements with five physical tests. An applicant had to climb a six foot wall, and do a six stair climb, up and back, three times. There was a physical restraint simulation, followed by a 600 foot race around scattered cones. Finally, the applicant had to drag a 170 pound dummy some 45 feet.

    The seven foot tall, Donte Clark breezed through the requirements on his first attempt, while Juanito Lewis just made it on his third and final try, and thus escaped a transfer to the city sanitation department. The six foot wall climb had been a real challenge for the four foot, eleven inch candidate, as would be firing range qualification.

UNDER THE BUS

Juanito didn't like noisy mufflers, thunder claps or fireworks. He also had trouble staying in the right lane on the rifle range.

After graduation, Donde became assigned to a Bronx precinct to spend the next two years walking a beat, while the bilingual Juanito spent his initiation years in The Queens, pounding a typewriter. Then as fate would have it, the two rookies made sergeant at the same time, and reunited as homicide detectives in Brooklyn.

Many cases would come their way over the next few years. Most were solved, a few perished in the dead file cabinet, such as the death of Sir Harry Wadsworth, who got run over one snowy Christmas Eve, in what friends and family called a gang related homicide.

T'was common knowledge that Wadsworth was up to his gold plated cufflinks in debt, and down on his luck in every casino Atlantic City had to offer. Tour bus drivers were on a first name basis with Sir Harry, and riders who made the trip from

KYLE KEYES

the Big Apple and back, turned a deft ear to his tales of rigged slot machines and crooked dealers.

The NYC Police Dept had no such choice. The Wadsworth family contacted a U.S. Senator who came down through the channels to apply pressure to all homicide divisions. A city wide hunt was launched to round up all known loan sharks, passive and lethal. No convictions developed, and the case eventually became yesterday's newspaper.

Ironically, Sir Harry's snowy body would never have surfaced, had Donde not pulled off the road to investigate what sounded like a *thump in the night.*

Now, as members of the Hobbs Creek Police force, Clark and Lewis would face a homicide challenge that would almost sink their careers. Fortunately, help would come in the quantum form of Olan Ford Chapman, aka The Vigilante.

UNDER THE BUS

Dedicated to Roger Rodriguez
N.Y. City, Sgt. Detective-retired.

KYLE KEYES

UNDER THE BUS

Chapter 1

Elizabeth Ghetti sat on her front room sofa, quietly loading bullets into a Smith & Wesson hand gun. Sunbeams ricocheted off Lake Powhattan, causing each shell to sparkle as the stony eyed woman stuffed the 22 caliber cartridges into the weapon's magazine holder. Off in the distance, sporadic rumbles warned of a storm brewing.

"Just don't be late," purred the slender woman to no one listening, "I do have other matters to tend before the sun goes down."

KYLE KEYES

A wall clock mounted over a noisy TV sounded four chimes, which meant Richard Ghetti would be leaving the Hobbs Creek bank and heading home, briefcase in hand, overcoat slung over one shoulder. The woman clicked off the TV and moved to the cabin's large picture window that overlooked the resort's blue water and white sandy beaches. Lake Powhattan truly was an oasis of nature. A local poet named Abigail Anderson phrased it best when she wrote: *Our park grounds are a rustic retreat in a nine to five world of stop lights and bridge tolls. Cabins surround our sparkling water like a frontier wagon train. Oak trees flutter with robins come spring. Squirrels rob seed from handy bird feeders, and a bold mallard might peck at our screen door for stale breadcrumbs.*

Elizabeth Ghetti shoved the magazine into the revolver and returned to the sofa. She did not like ducks. She did not like poetry, and she did not like Lake Powhattan. She set the gun down on the black and red, plaid cover and opened a large cell

UNDER THE BUS

phone. Richard Ghetti was not her first husband, but hopefully, he would not be her last.

Her first husband was a man named Happy George who was bald, owned a pot belly and a dozen used car lots scattered throughout Lower Elk County. Gossip had it that George was a millionaire–or maybe even richer, so she took a chance and married the guy, only to find out that his bankroll wheezed from more hot air than his sales pitch. TV ads don't come cheap and somehow the rotund, car lot owner checked out in the red instead of the green. His penis size was nothing to brag about either, and his dinner talk held the zest of re-heated meat and potatoes..

She held the phone at arm's distance and took a selfie. She examined the image and smiled. Her firm jawline, young skin and blue eyes made a great photo. And, much to the chagrin of jealous peers, her physique was near perfect but for an arm scar suffered while she held George's head under water. Fortunately for her, the preliminary hearing came back: *accidental drowning while in bathtub,* despite some raised eyebrows from dubious employees. One assistant manager went so far as to accuse her of premeditated murder, to which she replied, "Prove it."

Now, with meal ticket gone, Elizabeth went back to work at the Mount Loyal Gentleman's Club where she met Richard Ghetti who would become her new Mr Goldbar. Ghetti came from good stock, and planned to buy out the Hobbs Creek National Bank, with financial aid from three other backers. As the weathered adage goes, Richard pursued Elizabeth until she caught him, and the two moved into this log cabin overlooking Lake Powhattan. Richard Ghetti became bank president, and she became wife of a bank president.

Purred Elizabeth, "And my class voted me most likely to go nowhere."

She posted her selfie on social media with the following question, "To all my followers, this is my hair swung over my left shoulder. I will follow up with a pic of my hair over my right shoulder. Which do you like best? Please respond. This is

UNDER THE BUS

important to me."

A tiny wooden bird jumped out of the wall clock to rudely announce the time. *Four-thirty.*

Elizabeth Ghetti swore softly. Wouldn't you know, the bastard picked this day to run late. But then in all fairness, it was the day after a holiday, social distancing was in place, and these two items alone would cause bank lines to back up. She opened her social media link and quietly awaited an answer to her two posts when Richard Ghetti's car pulled into the driveway. She dropped the cell phone and picked up the firearm. Cabins around Lake Powhattan had been put in backwards so picture windows faced the water. Thus, streets were in the rear. Driveways were cobble-stone pads that separated addresses. Elizabeth could hear her husband's leather oxfords crunching along the cabin wall.

She took a deep breath.

Suddenly, he was inside.

"Honey, I'm forty," he exclaimed, "Can you believe it! I finally reached forty!"

KYLE KEYES

His shirt collar was open, his black tie loose. He dropped the briefcase by the front door and stepped inside when she opened fire.

The first shell caught Richard Ghetti in the right rib cage.

He gasped and clutched his chest.

His eyes widened in disbelief. His mouth opened as though to cry out, but no words came.

Elizabeth Ghetti methodically fired two more shots and Richard Ghetti spun to the floor.

She arose from the sofa and stood over the body. The left leg moved. She shot the leg. His left arm twitched. She shot the arm. Then she emptied the gun into the body and whispered, "Happy Birthday, sweet heart."

Blood began to seep onto the floor.

Her cell phone beeped.

T'was an answer to her post. The community liked her hair swung to the left side.

"So do I," she purred blowing smoke from the weapon, "Seems like we're all in agreement."

Chapter 2

Police Sergeants, Donde Clark and Juanito Lewis burst through the door of Cabin 18, as Ivy Chapman fed rabbits and refilled water bowls. Screamed the seven foot Donde, "Sergeants Clark and Lewis responding to your call, Ma'am. Just stand clear. We'll take over!"

The startled woman dropped the water pitcher.

A caged parakeet screamed.

Rabbits ran for cover.

Donde Clark held his police issued '38 with two hands, barrel pointed toward the ceiling. Stealthy, he moved into the kitchen, lowered the weapon to point in all directions simultaneously and yelled "All clear!" Seconds later, the four foot, eight inch Juanito slipped into the bedroom, pointed his weapon in all directions and shouted, "All clear." After which, Donde by-passed Juanito and cleared the second bedroom.

The cabin consisted of only four rooms and a bath that formed a loop. On the officers' third time around, the stocky Ivy Chapman broke a broom handle over a chair back and screamed, "Okay, enough is enough already. I'm sure by now we're all in agreement that the cabin is clear!"

Instantly, the Hobbs Creek law officers holstered their weapons.

"Not to mention you are scaring the shit out of the rabbits," continued Ivy Chapman, "And can I see some ID?"

"My apologies, ma'am," said Donde using a fore finger to push sunglasses back up a nose that was too small for his body, "But we can't be too careful now can we. After all, Olan Ford Chapman is America's most wanted fugitive."

"Olan Chapman!" cried Ivy, "What does my Olan have to do with this?"

News worthy people, like news worthy stories come with a price. This held true for Ivy Chapman, wife of the fore-mentioned, Olan

UNDER THE BUS

Chapman, aka Jesse Joe Jacks, aka Samuel Leroy McCoy, aka Calvin Cannonball Cooper, aka The Vigilante. Every gun shot, siren or flashing light would bring unwanted attention to the rustic doorstep of Cabin Eighteen..

In retrospect, Olan was wanted for countless killings, committed under the influence of a mental metamorphose known as D.I.D. (Dissociative Identity Disorder) formerly known as MPD (Multiple Personality Disorder). His eyes would change color. Amnesia would set in. Severe headaches often followed. During these blackouts, Olan Chapman became someone he once was. A being from another generation, another galaxy. another time warp. And always, someone who could handle impending danger. Dr Adler Dearwood who was Olan's life-long head shrink, blamed the eerie metamorphose on a childhood trauma that beset the Buffalo City schoolboy.

When he turned eight years old, Olan watched three high school boys rape his older sister, following a late night, cheerleader practice.

KYLE KEYES

The three boys dragged the girl behind some bushes and chased young Olan off with threats and a penknife. A school janitor found Olan the next morning, huddled behind a furnace in the school's boiler room. A ground search failed to turn up Olan's sister, Rebecca Ann Chapman, who still remains among the missing.

The Buffalo City psychologist also blamed Olan's heavy drinking and suicide attempts on that same ugly incident, stating that Olan felt somehow responsible for the heinous fate that befell his sister.

"I understand, ma'am," said Donde, "How ever, your husband is wanted for gunning down at least a hundred people."

"A hundred people?"

"Yes ma'am, a hundred people"

"Really?"

"Maybe two hundred," chimed in Juanito, "Or maybe even three hundred."

"Really officer, you must read the tabloids."

"Yes ma'am, and he is also a crack shot,"

UNDER THE BUS

"Then you best stay out of his gun sights," said Ivy, who knew that her husband had never fired any weapon in his life but a potato gun – and that was at a Sunday school picnic.

"Ma'am, we do represent the law," said Donde.

"Officer, Olan Chapman couldn't hit a bull in the ass with a ping pong paddle," said Ivy Chapman by way of admission, "The only thing my husband can shoot off is a firecracker on the 4th of July. And he only does that when I'm there to supervise."

"Yes ma'am," replied Donde Clark who had been fully briefed on the vigilante sightings, "But, when your husband, or his alter-ego kills someone, he becomes judge, jury and executioner, and that's against the law."

Ivy Chapman tried not to yawn. She studied law via a computer course entitled *Know Your Rights*, and was a big fan of Judge Judy, Ben Matlock, and early black/white episodes of Perry Mason. She retied a wrinkled apron and headed for the kitchen sink while saying, "Well, Olan's not here, Is there anything else, officers?"

"Yes ma'am," replied Donde, "We need to talk about the gunshots?"

"And we need to talk about all these rabbits?" broke in Juanito Lewis, "They must be in violation of some animal control code."

"I think we need to talk about the gunshots," said Ivy Chapman.

Dearwood was responsible for the rabbits. The Buffalo City psychologist felt the furry creatures would be good therapy for Olan's frazzled personality. Dear wood also recommended re-location, a suggestion that eventually brought the Chapman's from upper New York State to this pine tree setting in South Jersey – with a helping hand from fate.

The year was 2008. Olan worked for a gigantic computer firm when the layoff order came down from upstairs. The nation reeled from a stock market crash. Downsizing became a household word. America stayed home as gas prices soared,

UNDER THE BUS

and technology sales fell to an all time low.

Olan's first reaction to the pink slip was disbelief. Then he stopped by the local tap room to tie one on, and Lady Luck chose to smile on this Phi bet ta kappa with no children and two pet rabbits. He had no sooner found a sympathetic bar stool, when an ex-school mate named Marty Simmons sauntered in. Marty was a fellow computer geek who knew everybody who was hiring in Lower Elk County, N.J. A few drinks and a phone call later, the Chapman's were moving to Lake Powhattan, where Ivy did nothing but bitch, and Olan happily fed his rabbits who began multiplying faster than *after midnight* votes in a rigged election..

"My Uncle Ralph would have liked your husband," said Juanito Lewis returning a tan leather folder to an inside pocket, "Uncle Ralph was a crack shot like Mr Chapman and Uncle Ralph also raised rabbits and is that Timothy Hay . . it looks like Timothy Hay . .yes it is . .this is Timothy Hay!"

KYLE KEYES

Ivy Chapman looked down at Juanito crawling around on the floor, sampling fragments of rabbit food. She peered up at Sergeant Donde and barked, "Why is this officer wearing cowboy spurs in my house. He's gouging my new floor."

"Juan!" cried Donde, "Juan!"

Instantly, Juanito jumped to his feet and said, "I theek we need to talk about the gunshots, ma'am."

" I just had this floor put in!"

"My partner wears boots with lifts," said Donde Clark, "It makes him look taller."

"You don't need spurs to wear boots!"

"Yes ma'am," acknowledged Donde, "But we do need to talk about the gunshots and I'll talk to my partner about the spurs. We got a call from somebody who heard gunfire coming from this cabin."

"I made that call and the gunshots came from next door," cried out Ivy Chapman, "You are in the wrong cabin!"

"Next door?"

UNDER THE BUS

"Yes, next door. The gunshots came from Cabin Twenty. This is Cabin Eighteen."

"Juan, we are in the wrong cabin," cried Donde.

"Yes, this es the wrong cabin," agreed Juan, heading happily for the door.

"Tootle," said Donde.

"Tootle?" replied the woman.

   * * * * *

Ivy stood at the picture window and watched the two law officers run for their mode of transportation, a short bed pickup with monster-wheels and red hubcaps that glowed in the dark. A pair of jumbo dice hung from the mirror. A bumper sticker read: *Watch Our Rear End, We'll Watch Hers.* Juanito climbed a ladder to reach the passenger door. After which, Donde tossed the folding rungs into the back and jumped in the drivers seat.

The siren came on.

KYLE KEYES

Lights began flashing.

The truck bounced across the yard and skidded to a stop in front of Cabin Twenty. Donde slid out and propped the ladder up against the passenger door. Ivy Chapman reached for a wall phone as Juanito hustled down the ladder and touched ground.

"Isabel?"

"Yes ma'am?" queried Hobbs Creek's first black dispatcher.

"Put Chief Phillips on the phone."

"Chief Phillips is on the other line, ma'am."

Ivy swore softly. She stared at her damaged floor boards and then barked, "Isabel, get Chief Phillips off the other line and onto this line. I want to talk to him!"

Moments later, a strange voice sounded from the far end of the line.

"Who's this?" asked Ivy.

"Sergeant Miller, ma'am."

"Where's Chief Phillips?"

"He's on the other line."

UNDER THE BUS

"Where's Isabel?"

"She went to the ladies room, can I help you?"

"Do you have five thousand dollars?"

"No ma'am."

"Then get Chief Phillips on the phone!"

The heavy brown hair on Ivy Chapman's forearms bristled as she recounted to the police chief how her new flooring became damaged. She turned back to the window as Donde tossed the folding ladder into the pickup bed, and then led the way to the front door of Cabin Twenty.

"Their names are Donde Clark and Juanito Lewis," explained Phillips in response to Ivy's question, "They just joined our Hobbs Creek Police Force and we can't be anything but honored. Both men have a long and distinguished service record of solving homicide cases in the Big Apple."

"The Big Apple?"

"New York City."

"Of Course."

"Now, if you will," said the Hobbs Creek police chief, satisfied that Ivy Chapman had settled down, "Put Detective Sergeant Clark on the phone."

"Can't do that," replied the woman.

"And why not?"

"Detective Sergeant Clark and Detective Lewis are next door in Cabin Twenty."

"And why are Clark and Lewis next door?"

"Because that's where the fucking gunshots came from!!!"

Sudden silence fell, followed by an apology from the Hobbs Creek police chief who finished by saying, "Ivy, it was an honest mistake. We both know that your husband is wanted for multiple killings, which of course led us to this miss-assumption."

"And we also know," snorted Ivy Chapman, "That my Olan would only fight for Truth, Justice and The American Way."

"Yes ma'am."

Ivy Chapman slammed down the phone and

UNDER THE BUS

pushed a fuzzy rabbit away from her ankles. It hadn't always been like this. There was a time when she had someone other than rabbits for conversation. A time when she and Olan shared dinner, fun, arguments and the same bed. Then came the holiday car accident in which Olan suffered a head concussion, and when the bony computer wizard snapped out of the coma, he became a former ego from another era: a hero who would never drink or attempt suicide or run from danger; a steward of justice; a defender for the weak, the persecuted. Mild mannered, Olan Chapman would become - *The Vigilante.*

"I should have listened to mama," lamented Ivy, "She told me to stay out of bars."

The Chapmans first met at an Orange County bar in Kissimmee, Florida. They were in the Orlando area to visit Walt Disney's Animal Kingdom. The year was 2004. Six named hurricanes blew through the Sunshine State in less than three months. Floridians were frightened. You could see the apprehension in taunt faces at food markets, gas stations, supply centers where home owners flocked to buy bottled water and plywood. News media suggested that the Sunshine State be renamed the hurricane state. One isolated email wanted to move Florida north to Alaska.

    Hurricane Charlie was the second blow of that busy season. Charlie came ashore at Punta Gorda, raged through Zolfo Springs and stormed into Orange County before moving north. Winds clocked between 110 and 150 mph. State damages reached 13 billion, plus. Charlie also spawned sudden tornadoes, closed down Disney's Animal Kingdom, and landed Olan Chapman on a bar stool next to Ivy Ann Goya.

    "Nana, also warned me about bars," muttered Ivy as she pulled a hidden cell phone from a kitchen drawer. She flipped open the lid, dialed and said, "Olan, get your baggy ass home.!"

    "Ivy," said a distant voice, "You are not to call me. I'm supposed to call you. You know we can't afford to keep buying burners."

UNDER THE BUS

"Olan, there's been a shooting."

They married in a fever hotter than a Jalepeno pepper. They designated Hurricane Charley as their best man, and set up house keeping in a Buffalo City condo near Olan's work site. Two pay raises later, they bought a split level in Hyde Park not far from Niagara, where Olan went over the Falls in a barrel to raise public awareness of Male Dysfunctional Disorder.

"A shooting where?" asked the distant voice.

"Next door."

"Which next door?"

"Cabin Twenty."

"What happened?"

"I don't know," whispered the stocky woman as though someone was eavesdropping, "But whatever is going on, sooner or later the authorities will blame you, and you need to be here to defend yourself."

Chapter 3

    Detective Sergeants, Donde Clark and Juanito Lewis burst through the front door of Cabin Twenty to find Elizabeth Ghetti knelt over Richard Ghetti's life-less body. Screamed the seven foot Donde, "Just stand clear ma'am, we'll take over !"

  "They shot my huggy bear," sobbed America's newest widow snapping off a social media website and grabbing a nearby hanky, "My poor huggy bear."

    "Are they still in the building, ma'am?"

    "They shot my huggy bear," sobbed the distraught looking woman..

    Donde Clark had just cleared the kitchen of any imposing danger when he realized Officer Lewis was not behind him. He turned to see Junito laying face down next to Richard Ghetti. Yelled Donde to Elizabeth Ghetti, "Don't touch him, he suffers from hemaphobia and I can't predict what he might do."

"They shot my huggy bear," sobbed Elizabeth.

Hemaphobia is what the medical profession calls an *abnormal fear of blood.* This rare phobia is common among children and adolescents. Juanito Lewis came down with the affliction as a five year old witnessing a high-wire act that turned revengeful. As his Uncle Herbie flew toward the outstretched arms of wife and aerial partner, Aunt Tessie, the bitter woman pulled away and allowed her two-timing husband to fall head first into the circus cannon, some 30 ft below.

"Blood shot everywhere," explained Donde turning Juanito's head to remove a partial denture, "As I understand it, Uncle Herbie had something going on with the Fat lady behind the big top."

"I was in the tub when the men broke in and shot Richard," sobbed Elizabeth, "And today was his birthday. He turned forty years old, today. And now he's gone."

"Anyway, it really turned out to be the final act for Juan's Uncle Herbie," said Donde, "Not to mention a long jail sentence for Aunt Tessie."

The fatal high-wire act also closed the tent flaps on the Big Top Gala, a traveling circus based on eighty acres of South Jersey farmland, and owned by Juanito's grand parents, Raymond and Lolita Lewis. Juan's father was circus ring master, and Juan's mother kept the books and secured engagements as the Lewis' circus joined other carnival acts in a transition from outdoor tents to indoor stages. T'was the beginning of the *contemporary circus,* and the end of a hayseed era when a horse could outrun a car, and a schoolboy would run from reality to join the circus. Ironically, the contemporary Juanito Lewis ran away from the circus to join reality.

"And that's how I come to meet my little buddy, here," babbled Donde taking Juanito's pulse reading,, "We both attended the same New York City academy to become police officers and that's when we discovered that Juanito was also nato-natal, and I know you must be wondering what nato-natal is, so I won't keep you in suspense, nato-natal is a blood condition - no, not a blood type - but a blood condition which allows Juanito, and specimens like Juanito, to donate blood to an infant."

"We never had children," sobbed Elizabeth, "Richard wanted children but I wanted to wait, and now it's too late. . .huggy bear is gone."

Juanito Lewis could also speak fluid Spanish as well as English, which put the former circus midget behind a desk while Donde Clark walked a beat for the two years that is customary initiation procedure for raw rookies in New York City. Fact is, fate smiled on Juanito right from the get-go. Due to female applicants, the city had replaced height and weight requirements with five physical tests. An applicant had to climb a six foot wall, and do a six stair climb, up and back, three times. There was a physical restraint simulation, followed by a 600 foot race around scattered cones. Finally, the applicant had to drag a 170 pound dummy some

45 feet.

The seven foot tall, Donte Clark breezed through the requirements on his first attempt, while Juanito Lewis just made it on his third and final try, and thus escaped a transfer to the city sanitation department. The six foot wall climb had been a real challenge for the four foot, eight inch candidate, as would be the firing range qualification. Juanito did not like noisy mufflers, thunder claps or fireworks. He also had trouble staying in the right lane on the rifle range. But somehow with Clark's help, Lewis climbed to the rank of sergeant and would join Donde as a Big Apple, homicide detective.

"Damn!" cried Donde suddenly, "I think he's going into shock. . .he's shaking. . .his eyes are rolling around in his head!"

"He's staring at my tits!" cried Elizabeth closing an open robe that would not stay closed.

"You need to call 911," instructed Donde.

Elizabeth Ghetti stared at Sergeant Donde Clark. She swung her gaze down to Richard Ghetti growing colder by the minute. Blood now trickled

UNDER THE BUS

along the hard wood floor and began to seep onto Juanito Lewis' fallen body. She looked back to Donde and said in question form, "You want me to call 911."

"Yes," begged Donde, "Call 911!!!"

KYLE KEYES

Chapter 4

"Well, she called 911," said Chief Alvin Phillips, turning to stare out the second story window of the Hobbs Creek, police station.

Today, this headquarters' building is a three story glass and steel structure that replaced a farmhouse that served as Hobbs Creek's first police station. The ground level is reserved parking for employees and visitors. Top level is storage for parks and recreation equipment. Dispatch, top brass offices, along with interrogation, break rooms and a food court stretch across the second floor. Computers and forensic equipment fill in the nooks and crannies.

Alvin Phillips became top cop when Police Chief, Benjamin Little retired with a coronary condition known as Congestive Heart Failure. Little suffered from a leaky aorta valve that would not close properly, and consequently caused his heart

UNDER THE BUS

to exist in a state of Atrial fibrillation. Dr Samuel Irvine, who served as Hobbs Creek primary physician, nudged Little into retirement, which led Mayor Willard Green IV to appoint Phillips as police chief. Alvin was well liked by voters, and was a local boy who graduated from the Mt Loyal Police Academy, and then worked his way up through the ranks at nearby Carson City. Now, staring down at it all, the rotund middle-age man, understood the term, *the heat is on.*

Below, flashing squad cars lit the huge parking lot, now surrounded by barb wire fence. A fire truck chased an ambulance from the open firehouse that sat across the street. An unseen dog let out a howl to chime in with the sirens. Continued Phillips, "The lady also called the mayor, the newspapers and posted the event on social media. . .and Sergeant Lewis, I want you to get your spurs off my desktop!"

Donde Clark picked up Juanito and sat his tiny partner on a swivel chair between Sergeants' Miller and Hodges who finished the preliminary investigation while Clark and Lewis went to County General Hospital. Police Chief Phillips and the four detective sergeants were now attempting to piece together the chain of events that took place in Cabin Twenty at Lake Powhatan, the night Richard Ghetti was shot six times with a Twenty-Two caliber handgun.

"I'm puzzled by the phone calls," said Phillips, "We have the first call coming in at four-forty. That call came from Ivy Chapman who lives next door in Cabin Eighteen. Ms Chapman called because she heard gun shots. Now, we have the shooting call which came from Elizabeth Ghetti. However, this call didn't come in until four-fifty. I can't figure out what the lady was doing for ten minutes."

"She was in the tub," said Detective Sgt Leon Hodges from behind dark sunglasses, "And I wish to remind the chief that I'm off the clock. I'm only here because I happened to be in the area when the call came in."

"So noted," replied Chief Alvin Phillips,

UNDER THE BUS

"Now, getting back to the lady, it does not take ten minutes to walk from that bathroom to the living room – in this case, the front door. I've been in those cabins and they are not that big. Basically, just four rooms and a bath."

"I have the lady's statement," said Sgt Cy Miller who took a written statement from Elizabeth Ghetti while Leon Hodges poked around the cabin. Explained Cy Miller, "If this reads funny, Chief, it's because I wrote it as a quote in the first person."

"Understood," replied Alvin Phillips.

"I was tub bathing when I heard male voices in my front room. I reached for my cell phone and realized it wasn't with me. Sudden panic set in. Strange men were in my cabin. I eased from the tub and secured the latches on the bathroom door -

"Sergeant Miller?"

"Yeah Chief."

"Is this a statement or a short story?"

T'was no mystery that Sergeant Cy Miller held dreams of early retirement to a bay side house on Long Beach Island, where the bald headed bachelor would fish away the hours, writing murder mysteries. And lo and behold, here was a murder mystery dumped right into his lap. Continued Miller, " I heard my husband's car pull into the driveway. You can see my dilemma, a beautiful, naked woman in a bathtub with gunmen lurking outside my door."

"Miller, who used the adjective *beautiful*, you or the lady?"

"The lady, chief."

"Go on."

"Anyway, with no phone, Mrs Ghetti had no way to warn her unsuspecting husband that danger awaited inside the cabin, Seconds seemed like minutes. Minutes seemed like hours. Then gunshots rang out-

"Miller !"

"Yes ,Chief?"

"Can we cut to the chase, here?"

"Yes Chief . .after the gunshots, the lady could not be sure if the gunmen left," said Miller,

UNDER THE BUS

"Therefore, she did not hurry out to the front room to investigate, and that accounts for the time lapse between the phone calls."

"So noted," replied Phillips.

"Thank you, Chief."

Alvin Phillips burped, patted a belly that lapped over his belt and took a phone call. His round black eyes stared back at a deer head that protruded from a paneled wall with no windows. He hung up the phone and rocked back in the squeaky desk chair that came with the territory. Both the deer head and the rocker were reminders of William Bo Brennan who became Hobbs Creek's first Police chief on December 4, 1949.

Supposedly, Brennan was the strongest man in Lower Elk County, which is how this backwoods trapper got to be Police Chief. Tales of Brennan's strength range from a fishy odor to sheer flap doodle. It's said he once rolled a getaway car upside down with his bare hands, then used a jack handle to cuff the holdup man to a door post. In another incident, he tossed an entire motorcycle gang out Binky's Liquor Store with no back up call. Corky Tabor, a connoisseur of wines, whiskeys and cough syrup, claims he saw Brennan hand brace a broken timber under the Cedar Gap Bridge while a runaway fright train crossed to safe ground.

Pure or colored, the stories graced Brennan until his 1977 retirement party, at which time the legendary police chief was replaced by First Lieutenant Adam Quayle, who gave way to Alvin Phillips predecessor, Benjamin Little.

Phillips stopped trying to out stare the deer head on the wall, and gazed at a metal serving tray covered with loose sugar and dried coffee stains. Phillips did not like hunting and fishing and trapping. Alvin Lee Phillips loved *the great indoors.* He loved desk duty and he loved to sip coffee. He eyed an empty mug that said *Chief* and thought about calling the dispatch desk.

Bad idea.

Isabel Jackson was on duty and Alvin Phillips and Jackson were not coffee mates. Jackson was the former Isabel Brown who suffered a hearing

UNDER THE BUS

loss while working for an upstate port authority. T'was one of those *wrong place* at the *wrong time* things. As Isabel collected bridge fare, a wrinkled lady with a large bugle blew out her right ear drum, and that would be the first of three mishaps to befall Isabel in a year's time. Her daughter got knocked up by a white boy, and her husband ran off with the boy's mother to audition for Dancing With The Stars.

Things brightened the following year. Isabel met Boa Beans Jackson who served as a Lower Elk County lawyer. Beans was not interested in chasing down the Mister Brown, but his bespectacled eyes sparkled hearing the words *port authority*. He married Isabel and kept her public name as Mrs Brown until after the pending trial. Thus far, the libel case has been delayed because port authority lawyers can't find a wrinkled lady with a large bugle.

Meanwhile, Jackson secured a civil service job for Isabel as Hobbs Creek's first black dispatcher. She broke in under former police chief,

KYLE KEYES

Benjamin Little, and was behind the duty desk when Alvin Phillips arrived on the scene. .and. . Isabel Brown Jackson lost no time drawing a line in the sand. She did not run errands, empty trash, shine shoes, or fix coffee.

"Sir," said Sergeant Miller interrupting Phillips walk down memory lane, "Would you like me to fetch some coffee from the kitchen?"

"Thank you, Miller."

Before the coffee arrived, Hobbs Creek mayor, Willard J. Green IV showed up in black swimming trunks and beach sandals. His fat eyes boiled. His porky face glowed from sun and anger. He shoved the morning paper under Phillips nose and fingered the headline that read: *Hobbs Creek Cop Faints At Sight Of Blood.*

Hobbs Creek has seen many changes over the decades, other than this steel and glass structure that stands at the corner of Elm and Main Streets. Millie's Meat Market gave way to a shopping mall just outside town proper limits. Otto's Farm And Garden bit the dust due to a

UNDER THE BUS

highway by-pass that detoured prospective customers around the once popular fruit and vegetable mart. Old Man Mayo's Esso is now an Exxon Mobil station with today's sticker shock prices, and Barney Kibble's taxi cab service evolved into Tri County Taxi with cabs that actually make an effort to stop for red lights.

Somethings never change.

The mayor of Hobbs Creek has always been a Willard J. Green, and down through the generations, each Willard Green has worn black swimming trunks, paddled around in sandals and owned some beachfront property – which makes many residents wonder what happens with their tax money. Willard J Green IV was no different than his predecessors. Also, this fourth edition of Mayor Green would spit saliva through an opening in his front teeth when upset or excited, which he was right now.

"Phil, I hope you realize that Hobbs Creek is the laughing stock of the county," cried Green, "No, we are the laughing stock of the nation and I want this man removed from the force!"

Phillips paused to wipe saliva off a desk calendar and then locked eyes with Willard Green to softly say, "Your Honor, the man we speak of stands behind you, if you would like to tell him yourself."

There are moments that live in infamy. December 7, 1941: Pearl Harbor day. July 20, 1969 when Neil Armstrong set foot on the moon. This was yet another one of those moments. As Willard J Green IV turned to look down at Juanito Lewis, air came out of the city hall dignitary like a wine bottle with the cork pulled.

"I'm Sergeant Lewis," said Juanito.

"Oh," replied Green who envisioned himself as a champion who fought for equal rights for all voters, regardless of race, religion or physical handicaps.

"I suffer from Hemaphobia." ?

"Oh."

"My twin brother also has this affliction, we think it might be hereditary."

UNDER THE BUS

"You have a twin brother?" broke in Phillips, "I don't recall seeing that mentioned in your dossier."

"Juanito has a brother named Joshua," verified Donde, "Sometimes, April and I have them over for dinner. Currently, Joshua is in Montana purchasing a dude ranch."

"Really?" said Mayor Willard Green, suddenly finding his voice, "That must take some coins."

Joshua and Juanito Lewis were of Quaker descent, and as most folks know, Quakers were detailed record keepers. These early American settlers recorded birth, death, marriage, tree markers, etc, etc. Unfortunately, these passive people would often get run off their land.

Now, after years of research and with some legal help, Joshua Lewis was ready to take back what rightfully belonged to George William Lewis and his descendants -namely, Manhattan Island.

Willard Green stared down at Juanito Lewis, and then at Donde Clark who stared at Alvin

KYLE KEYES

Phillips who stared at Juanito Lewis who stared back at Willard Green, who stared at Alvin Phillips, who stared at the ceiling fan and muttered, *Beam Me Up Scotty.* After which, Green quietly picked up his news paper and found his way out.

"Later?" called out Phillips.

"Later," replied Green.

The coffee arrived just ahead of Sgt Kelsey Springer who headed Hobbs Creek's forensic's unit. As previously stated, Hobbs Creek is not The Big Apple. Sgt Springer was equipped with one giant flash bulb camera, a Sherlock Holmes magnifying glass, and a fingerprint kit that looked like it came from a nickel and dime store. The Hobbs Creek Police Station was built in the early Eighties, when fingerprints were still sent to the county seat for verification, and micro chip technology meant little to builders or bureaucrats.

"I did get four good print sets," said Springer, pushing his cart center stage before erecting a screen and projector, "The prints belong to Richard Ghetti, Elizabeth Ghetti, Donde Clark and Juanito Lewis. If anyone else was in the

UNDER THE BUS

cabin, they wore gloves."

To Springer's credit, the thirty year old police academy, graduate could run a Uhlenhuth test to determine human blood from animal blood, analyze DNA, match up hand and foot prints, and for all who would listen, Springer would gladly recount his two year lab experience working under Mt Loyal medical examiner, Dr Erwin Campbell.

"Can we roll the pictures?" asked Phillips.

"Pictures we have," replied Kelsey Springer eagerly rolling through dozens of images that covered every nook and cranny in the cabin, "I also have pictures of the bathroom, and as you can see, there is water in the tub."

"And that checks with the lady's story," pointed out Sergeant Miller.

"Springer, is there some reason you have more pictures of Mrs Ghetti than you have of the victim?"

"She kept standing in front of my lens, Chief."

"Of course," growled Phillips, "Can we back up to the gun case?"

KYLE KEYES

Richard Ghetti's gun rack was a varnished maple box mounted over the front room sofa. The case held two weapons, a Colt 38 and a Smith & Wesson 45, which were locked behind a glass door. Richard Ghetti had *concealed carry* permits for both guns.

"I assume the Mrs Ghetti unlocked the case for you," queried Phillips.

"She did," confirmed Springer, "Neither weapon had been fired and as we know, neither weapon is a Twenty Two."

"So, here's what got," said Alvin Phillips addressing the group, "Person or persons unknown, surprised Mr Richard Ghetti upon arriving home, shot the victim six times with a caliber 22 pistol, then disappeared leaving no trace of fingerprints, foot prints or tire tracks. The victim's wife saw nothing but her dead husband lying just inside the front door. Thus, we have an APB (all points bulletin) out there with little to go on."

Juanito Lewis slid off his leather office perch

UNDER THE BUS

with toes stretching to reach the floor. He stepped to the viewing screen and commandeered Sgt Springer's picture pointer. Said Lewis in flat *matter of fact* tones, "You can call off the APB (all points bulletin), Chief. Elizabeth Ghetti killed Richard Ghetti."

"Really," replied Alvin Phillips, "And what did you see that the rest of us missed?"

Juanito Lewis pushed the *viewers* back button and stopped on a picture of a rug folded over a chair. He used the pointer to high light the small area carpet designed to be an entrance mat. Said Juanito, "Mrs Chapman who lives next door has this very same rug."

"Interesting, Sergeant Lewis," replied Phillips, "So Ms Ghetti and Ms Chapman shop the same store. They may even shop together. Any thing else?"

"But Mrs Chapman has her rug just inside the entrance way where it belongs."

"So maybe Mrs Ghetti was cleaning the floor," suggested Alvin Phillips.

"Maybe," said Donde Clark backing up his partner, "But somehow, I don't think Elizabeth Ghetti cleans anything but her hair and her fingernails."

Alvin Phillips swung the screen around for a better look. He ran a forefinger over his tiny lip mustache and stared intently at Juanito Lewis. "So where are we going with this, Sergeant?"

"This is what we call Murder One back in New York City, Chief. Premeditated. Well executed. Little or no clues. Elizabeth Ghetti knew when she was going to shoot her husband. She knew where she was going to shoot him. She knew where the body was going to fall. Her new entrance rug is folded over that window chair because she didn't want it blood stained."

"Interesting," said Phillips.

"Yes, interesting," agreed Sgt Miller.

"Interesting, but pretty thin," pointed out Sgt Kelsey Springer who saw rainbows in black and white, "You got anything else?"

UNDER THE BUS

Alvin Phillips paused to take a phone call, then locked eyes with Juanito. Said Phillips in flat tones, "You want a chance to redeem yourself, sergeant?"

"Yes he does," replied Donde.

"Okay, you two go back out to Cabin Twenty and check the status of that throw rug," said Phillips, "I want verification on what she uses it for."

"Can we get a legal search warrant? asked Donde.

"No chance."

"Well, we can't just barge in," said Donde, "The initial investigation is over."

Chief Phillips went back to his thinking post at the smudgy glass window that overlooked the parking lot below. He placed two hands on the window sill, and watched a gray haired lady smack a would-be purse snatcher with a handbag that held a two pound black jack. The assailant dropped to his knees in time to take a nose full of pepper spray. After which, the granny shot him with a stun gun.

The assailant was someone Lower Elk County authorities had been after for a year. The granny was an undercover cop. Phillips came away from the window muttering, "Undercover. .yes . we will go undercover."

"Chief, have you gone bonkers," snickered Sgt Miller, "We can't send these two undercover. They look like Mutt and Jeff."

UNDER THE BUS

Chapter 5

Elizabeth Ghetti just finished drawing her second bath of the day when the doorbell rang. She shut down the hot water mix, threw on a housecoat and grabbed her cell phone. A message awaited. A follower liked her last post which showed her new purple, painted finger-nails. She smiled and replied, "Yes, I like them myself."

The doorbell rang again.

She tied the housecoat securely around her waist swung open the door and cried, "Yo ho, and what do we have here?"

Donde Clark and Juanito Lewis stood framed in the doorway, disguised as vacuum cleaner salesmen. Each man wore a black, handlebar mustache, and held a dust buster with all the attachments. Juan's hose attachment bounced off the porch floor boards.

KYLE KEYES

"We're not here on police business," lied Donde "This is our moonlighting job."

"Of course," smiled the widow.

"You veel love my vacuum," said Juan, "All of the attachments are made with this new plastic material that doesn't wear, tear or collapse. It's a new product the government uses in space ships. We use it here on Earth for plumbing pipes and vacuum cleaners."

"Let me guess," said Elizabeth, "You want to come in, sprinkle dirt everywhere, and then demonstrate the awesome pickup power of your dust busters."

"Something like that," said Donde.

Hobbs Creeks' newest widow lit a cigarette and blew smoke at the two police officers, while explaining she had no plans to take a space trip with a vacuum cleaner. Then she used the F word to kiss them goodbye, and slammed closed the door.

*   *   *   *   *

UNDER THE BUS

An hour later, Donde Clark and Juanito Lewis were back. They bumped heads against an unyielding windshield, as their 4x4 came to an abrupt stop at the porch steps to Cabin Twenty.

Dust balls rose from beneath the monster wheels amid a sickening sound of broken wood.

"Okay Juan, here's Plan B," said Clark from behind the steering wheel, "We go in like we a have a right to be there. We don't ask to enter.. As soon as the lady answers the door, we just barge right in."

"I theek you heet the banister rail," said Sgt Lewis.

"It's these new glasses," explained Clark, "I can't get used to trifocals without lines."

"I hope the lady left home," said Juan.

Clark killed the siren and snapped off the bubble gum lights. He slid down to ground level, pulled a step ladder from the truck bed and propped the top rung against the passenger door step so his partner could climb down. Explained Clark playing rat-a-tat-tat with a brass knocker,

"Remember Juan, we have no business being here."

"We could leave now," suggested Juanito staring at the busted porch railing.

"The rug is there, Juan."

"You saw the rug?"

"I think I saw the rug."

"You theek you saw the rug?

"Just have your camera ready."

Suddenly, the front door swung open to reveal Elizabeth Ghetti, still wrapped in the bath robe that kept flashing open. Her purple toenails were dry, as was her shiny, brown ear-sweep. Said the woman in snappy tones, "I hope this is more important than my hair, I was just stepping into the shower."

"You seem to spend a lot of time in the bath room," noted Donde Clark.

The door slammed closed.

"Ma'am, we are police officers!"

The door opened.

UNDER THE BUS

"I'm Detective Sergeant, Juan Lewis and this is Detective Sergeant, Donde Clark," blurted out Donde Clark, "Code requires us to introduce ourselves each time we enter a crime scene"

"I think you mean you are Sergeant Clark and this is Sergeant Lewis," corrected the widow, "And you are not coming in."

"Juan will take off his spurs," promised Donde staring at a pair of exposed nipples.

"Spurs or no spurs, you are not coming in and why is that little creep taking pictures of my legs?"

"Turn your cell off," said Donde to Juan, then turning to Elizabeth Ghetti, "We could get a warrant."

"I don't think so," countered the woman, "This case has already moved from *active* to *ongoing*."

"You've talked to Judge Lampi?"

"Jules Lampi and my husband rode the same golf cart from time to time, and Tori Conners will be getting a bill for my busted railing."

"I don't know any Tori Conners," said Clark.

"Conners is our township clerk," explained the widow, "You *out of towners* are all the same, why don't you unpack your bags and move in."

Donde Clark was halfway through an apology for driving into the porch railing when Elizabeth Ghetti slammed the cabin door closed for a second time. Asked Clark as the two lawmen climbed back into the pickup, "Did you get the picture?"

"Right before she closed the door," replied Juanito Lewis.

"And?"

"It's the entrance rug that was folded over the window chair, when Richard Ghetti was gunned down."

"Let's see," said Clark taking the camera phone from his partner, "Yes, I see."

"Donde, you are looking at the lady's legs."

"Juan, just give me a minute, I'm working my way down to. . .the. . .mat . . .yes . .you are right. . .it is the same entrance rug."

UNDER THE BUS

"And it es the same entrance mat that the lady next door, has."

"And how does that happen?"

"Yes," echoed Juanito Lewis, "How does that happen?"

Chapter 6

Ivy Goya Chapman watched through parted curtains as Sgts Clark and Lewis climbed into the monster-wheel pickup and backed away from Cabin 20. Donde circled two scrub oaks supporting a hammock that belonged to the late Richard Ghetti, narrowly missed a cement bird bath that needed a bath, and headed toward Cabin 18.

Ivy groaned and with fingers crossed, headed for the front door. Outside, nature also greeted the newcomers. The squirrels and the blue jays battled over Ivy's side-yard bird feeder. Duffy's bull dog chased Murray's cat beneath Donde's pickup. Down at lakeside, a male mallard held a female's head under water until passionate splashes returned to dormancy. Said Ivy to Donde,

"You can come inside with your questions, but Shorty here stays on the porch."

"I'll have Officer Lewis remove his spurs," offered Clark.

UNDER THE BUS

"He stays outside !"

"Yes, ma'am," conceded Sgt Clark staring down at the oriental entrance mat that matched the rug next door, "I do have a couple more questions."

"So ask."

"When your neighbor Richard Ghetti was shot, you heard the gunfire?"

"I believe that's in the statement I gave the other two officers."

"Yes, ma'am," replied Clark, "I read your statement back at the station house. You heard six gunshots."

"That's what I heard."

"It could not have been four or five?" asked Clark, "Sometimes with gun fire, it's hard to count the rounds."

"I heard six shots," repeated Ivy, "The shots were slow and deliberate, as though . . . ."

"Ma'am. . .as though what?"

Ivy Chapman paused to look at Cabin 20 and then concluded, "As though the killer found some sort of enjoyment in killing Richard."

Clark pushed a white rabbit with pink eyes off his black oxfords and brushed a hair ball from his shoelaces to the floor. He asked permission to wash up at the kitchen sink and between sneezes, asked, "Did Richard Ghetti have many enemies?"

"I know Elizabeth much better than I knew her husband," said Ivy, "And why is Officer Lewis doing headstands on my front porch?"

"Officer Lewis likes to pretend he's back at the circus occasionally," explained Donde. Then, "Just one more question."

"Yes?"

"Did you see any strangers around the Ghetti cabin prior to Richard Ghetti coming home from work?"

"No."

"No strange cars . .hikers. . maybe someone fishing?"

"We don't fish in this lake."

Suddenly, Juanito lost balance and toppled into the brass dinner bell that hung from the porch

UNDER THE BUS

rafters. Bunny rabbits came from all directions. Big rabbits, baby rabbits, white rabbits, brown rabbits, trio-colored rabbits.

"I thought Animal Control rounded up all these rabbits," said Donde Clark lifting Juanito into the truck.

"I'm afraid the rabbits are more elusive than my husband," smiled the wife of America's Most Wanted fugitive.

Donde Clark lowered the driver's window for one more question. "If anything else comes to mind, will you call us . .anything, no matter how small."

Ivy Chapman nodded affirmative. Then peering down from the high porch deck into the truck cab, she said, "And now I have a question for you."

"Listening."

"Why are you officers sitting on your seat belts?"

"To keep them quiet," explained Donde, "The trick is to lock them across the seat and sit

69

on them. It stops those annoying little buzzer noises."

    Ivy Chapman stared blankly at Donde,
    No smile came.
    She stared at Juanito who began to whistle.
    She turned and went inside.

    *   *   *   *   *

Sometime later:
    "Elizabeth?"
    "Speaking."
    "Ivy here."
    "Yes?"
    "You shot him, didn't you?"
    "What !
    "You shot Richard."
    "Ivy, you don't know what you're saying."
    "Elizabeth, I know you. You killed Richard. . . and on his birthday."
    "Ivy !!! Why would I kill Richard?"
    "I don't know why, but I know you did it. There was no other person or persons here on that

UNDER THE BUS

day when Richard was killed. . .and I don't recall hearing or seeing a car leave."

"Ivy . . .I think from now on you better find someone else to take you shopping."

Chapter 7

Forty-eight hours later, despite additional data from Ivy Chapman and doormat conjecture from Officer Juanito Lewis, Case #40781477 (The Richard Ghetti Homicide) went on the back burner in the Hobbs Creek Police files.

UNDER THE BUS

Chapter 8

An empty oil drum and a rusty bull dozer welcome visitors to Pykes Pit. Sometimes, fallen tree limbs or a nosy pine snake will block the winding entrance road. Heavy foliage delays the dawn. Dense fog lingers in low areas.

Police Chief Alvin Phillips drove warily, ready for addled deer that might take aim at oncoming head-lights. A department issued .38 filled his side holster. A 410 shot gun rode in the passenger seat.

Pykes Pit lies roughly two miles northeast of Lake Powhatan, and some fifty yards inside a weaving Lower Elk Township border. To the southwest run the Atlantic City power lines that feed civilization to the desolate pine trees. To the northwest stretches the Elk County Game Forest, a forty square-mile tract that provides free camping, fishing and hunting. The tract joins the Pine Barrens. Rabbit and deer are abundant. Random rifle shots can be heard year 'round, despite a New Jersey State gaming timetable. Often, a folded doe gets quickly crammed into a ready car trunk. Occasionally, a poacher gets collared by the county game warden.

Phillips frowned and double checked all window and door locks.. He did not hunt, trap or fish, and he had no wish to swap campfire tales of Bigfoot, Black Lagoon creatures or the Jersey Devil, a green faced demon delivered to a Mrs. Leeds of Atlantic County's, Estelville,

By the Devil, himself.

One such story goes that after bearing a dozen healthy babies, the woman became pregnant by fooling around in the barnyard. Thus, the Devil delivered a deformed creature who would gain notoriety as The Jersey Devil. Born to be an outcast, the creature grew up in coastal swamp lands, beyond the reach of truant officers and table manners. Various sightings depict the demon as a vampire, a large bird, a kangaroo, a grizzly and a horse with bat wings. Almost every South Jersey native has either seen or heard of the devil. Since the late Eighteen Hundreds, his calling card has been a hoof print left in the sand, and a blue mist that precedes his appearance.

Despite the scary tales, many New Jersey natives paint the devil more saint than sinner, oddly enough. They credit the creature with scaring schoolboys to obey curfew laws, and inducing grownups to walk the straight and narrow as an atonement for Mrs Leeds' carnal misbehavior.

Thus, Elk County folk believe the devil patrols the Pine Lands, swinging a vengeful hammer of justice, while stomping out forest fires and wiping graffiti off grave markers. Regardless of motives good or evil, Phillips kept one hand on the shotgun and both eyes on the road ahead, looking for any signs of a blue mist.

He bounced the low-slung car over a one wagon bridge and through a cluster of white birches. Angry gravel chunks smacked the under carriage. Scrub branches lashed the windshield. He skirted a wide puddle and paused on a clearing that sloped upward toward a hidden cliff. Male voices filtered up from the basin floor, broken by spurts of gunfire."

He peered over the cliff's edge.

The voices belonged to Sergeants' Donde Clark and Juanito Lewis, who were zeroed in on a paper bulls eye plastered on a muddy basin wall.

Phillips breathed a sigh of relief and opened his cell phone to say, "They are here."

"I told you they would be there, suh."

"Yes Isabel," conceded Phillips, "You said they would be here."

The pit began as a hole in the ground when a post-war contractor named Lucas O'Leary began digging foundation dirt for a housing develop-ment called Bayside Glen. By the time the meadow lands project was finished, O'Leary's front-end loader had left a cavity big enough to bury the national debt, and house a target range large enough to satisfy shooting requirements for tournament sportsmen and local police officers seeking gun qualification.

UNDER THE BUS

Clark and Lewis were here to practice for gun qualification.

Phillips pocketed the cell phone and peered at a hovering black crow fleeting through the jagged rays of a rising sun. A white sandy path descended to the basin floor. Phillips grabbed a file folder from the passenger seat, and was halfway down the path when Juanito squeezed off a shot at the paper target. The crow fell from the sky and landed at Juanito's feet.

"Holy shit!" cried Phillips.

"Donde," cried Lewis.

"Oh damn!" cried Clark.

"Donde," whimpered Lewis.

"Juan, don't look up" whispered Clark grabbing his partner's quivering gun hand, "And don't look down. Just keep looking at the target."

"I don't believe what I just saw," cried Phillips, "That man just shot the crow out of the air, and he never once looked up. What a shot."

"It's bleeding isn't it?" mumbled Lewis, "The bird is bleeding."

KYLE KEYES

"Juan, just listen to me," whispered Clark, "Don't look down and don't look up. Keep your eyes on the target and very slowly. . .lower your arm . . .and return your weapon to it's holster."

"I've heard stories that New York City, police officers are expert marksmen," exclaimed Phillips walking up with the file folder outstretched, "Frankly, I never would have believed it if I hadn't seen it."

"Well, seeing is believing," replied Sgt Clark taking the file folder from Phillips, "And what is this?"

"The Ghetti case is back on the front burner."

"Oh?"

"This folder came in the mail," said the Hobbs Creek top cop, "It's from a Ms Jeffery Hanson, first name Anita . . and this does shed new light on an otherwise dead end case."

Clark slowly turned Juanito away from the fallen bird and then thumbed through the file folder. A dozen spread sheets were stapled page to page. A small note book was paper clipped to the

UNDER THE BUS

sheets. All the material bore the logo of a bank in Switzerland. Asked Clark, "So what's her story, Chief.?"

"Embezzlement," said Phillips, "The Ms Hanson found this stuff while cleaning out her husband's den. Richard Ghetti was bank manager but only part owner. He had three silent partners unknown to the general public. Mr Hanson was one of those partners as well as being book keeper."

"And she thinks her husband was skimming money off the top and sending it to Switzerland," said Donde guessing, "So why is she throwing his ass under the bus?"

Alvin Phillips took back the spread sheets, burped loudly, then stuffed the file folder beneath his belt in preparation for the long climb back out of the pit. He gave the dead bird one more glance and said, "I only talked to the lady on the phone, but she kept referring to her husband as that lying, cheating bag of shit."

"Oh."

"Yeah oh. . and I still can't believe that shot Juan made in dropping that bird. What a hell of a shot ! I'm surprised he's not doing any of his back over flips."

"They will come later," said Donde, "Right now, he needs to sit down and why aren't we bringing this Ms Hanson in for questioning?"

"She disappeared."

"Wow!" whistled Donde, "This plot thickened fast."

"When I had the lady on the phone," explained Phillips, "She indicated that her husband may have killed Richard Ghetti, and she felt that her own life was in danger. I have Isabel putting together a dozier of relatives and friends where she might stay,

"Meanwhile, I want you and Sgt Lewis to question Hanson's neighbors and co-workers."

UNDER THE BUS

Chapter 9

Further investigation cleared Jeffery Hanson of killing Richard Ghetti, due to testimony from more than a half dozen employees, who were with the bookkeeper at the time when the bank president was shot. However, the case made fresh headlines with the possibility that embezzlement was involved.

UNDER THE BUS

Chapter 10

Fosters Funeral Home was the sole mortuary for Hobbs Creek. The seven thousand, square foot morgue did burials, cremations and housed two sitting rooms for viewing and services. If more than two Hobbs Creek residents died in the same time window, a giant freezer in the crematory held the extra body. Elizabeth Ghetti sat in a front row seat of the main viewing room, a few feet from the casket that held Richard Ghetti. An over-head fan told her to don a sweater. A cell phone beep signaled an incoming message. She replied to the text and was halfway into a white knitted slip-on when a man entered the viewing room. She shut down the cell phone and whispered, "Thank you for coming."

The man nodded and knelt on one knee beside the casket. He was dressed to the nines and after rising, he rubbed an imaginary dust spot from his suit pants. A distant organ played *Faith Of Our Fathers Living Faith* and he made the sign of the cross before sitting down.

"I'm am surprised you came," said the woman.

"I wanted to make sure he was dead."

"How could he not be dead," scoffed Elizabeth Ghetti, "I plugged him six times."

The man was Jeffery Hanson. His name should have been handsome, because that he was. Wavy hair, deep face dimples and all that charisma stuff. He sat now with head down and hands clasped between knees as he whispered, "I wish there had been some other way."

"There was no other way," snapped the widow in hushed tones, "Just be thankful that I had the guts to throw his pathetic ass under the bus."

"But I feel so guilty," said Hanson staring down at an open shoelace, "It's almost as though I pulled the trigger."

UNDER THE BUS

"You are guilty," said Elizabeth, "You told me how to do it, and you bought the gun. . .does your wife suspect?"

"She found our Swiss account."

"Damn!" muttered Elizabeth.

"It's my fault," admitted Hanson, "I should have had it under lock and key."

"We need that account, Jeffery. . move it."

"Move it where?"

"I don't know," replied the widow, "You're the banker."

The Ghetti's and the Hansons met at an annual *Chilli Cook Off* hosted by Lake Powhattan. Applicants had to supply grilles, fuel and food. Judges were chosen from a notoriety list of which bank president, Richard Gehtti was a member. Sometime, during the all-night gala, Elizabeth and Jeffery's eyes locked, and destiny began to unravel. Richard Ghetti desired to buy the local bank, but needed more funds and a fresh bookkeeper. Hanson was a bookkeeper by trade and commandeered enough equity to become twenty-five percent owner. The other two partners showed up in the persons of Howard Dixon and Emerson Cook. Howie Dixon was the entrepreneur who transformed Otto's 100 acre fruit farm into endless rows of highrise condos, while Emerson owned and operated *Cookies* big rig towing service, which covered Lower Elk County and responded to roadside accidents that could not be handled by standard tow trucks.

Cookies was big. His two tow trucks ran well over six figures. His insurance bills could jolt Wall Street. And when cash flow was down, just buying those giant truck tires required a bank action, which is why everyone at Hobbs Creek National knew Cookie and addressed him as Mr Cook.

"Speaking of the devil," said Jeffery Hanson, "Here's the big man, now."

Emerson Cook burst into Fosters like a summer-time tornado dropping in on the bible belt. He went straight for the casket, made the sign of the cross and dropped down on one knee. He removed a ten gallon cowboy hat and stroked his

UNDER THE BUS

handlebar mustache before bowing his head to pray.

"I always suspected Emerson was bald," whispered Jeffery Hanson.

"You didn't know?" asked Elizabeth Ghetti.

"He would never take the hat off," replied Hanson, "Even at meals and meetings."

He's coming this way," whispered the widow, "I think you better leave. . .and pull yourself together."

The two man shook hands, after which Emerson dropped into the vacant seat.

"Thank you for coming," said Elizabeth.

"I just wanted to make sure he was dead," replied Emerson, "And who's the midget taking pictures?"

"Detective Sergeant, Juanito Lewis," replied the widow, "He transferred here from New York City. He's fascinated with my legs."

"Really?"

"Really."

"Why's he hiding behind the organ?"

"He thinks that I can't see him," replied

Elizabeth Ghetti, "He also thinks that I murdered Richard."

"You did murder Richard."

"He can't prove that," said the widow, "And neither can you."

"You want me to toss his ass out of here?"

"No," replied the lady dressed in black as she hit the video button on her cell phone, "I'll handle this."

"I haven't seen much of you lately," said Cook.

"I've been busy," explained Elizabeth, "We will get together as soon as the heat is off."

"We better," muttered Emerson Cook, "Just remember I know where the bodies are buried."

Chapter 11

Juanito Lewis went skipping up the back stairway to the Hobbs Creek, Police Station. His classified phone bounced from a holding strap hung around his neck. His tiny feet couldn't wait to reach the second level. He was just about to side step the dispatch cage when Isabel Brown put his brakes on.

"Alvin is gunning for you," said Hobbs Creek's first black dispatcher.

"But, I need to show him what I've got," cried Juanito.

"And he wants to show you something," said Isabel Brown.

Juanito found Chief Alvin Phillips staring out the second floor window at the busy intersection below. A fire alarm had squad cars, an ambulance, a tanker and a ladder truck scurrying in all directions. A man with a walker just missed a truck bumper, and a shabby dog lowered his leg long enough to let out a howl, and then scamper off. Cried Juanito waving his camera, "Chief, I've got something big here!"

"You do, huh?"

"I do !"

"Juanito, I want you to climb off my desk and sit in a chair," growled Phillips without turning around, "When your partner gets here, I've got something to show you two, if I can get Springer off his duff."

"Chief, this can't wait."

"It can wait."

Sgts Springer and Clark arrived together, only to prove that two grown men and a push cart can't squeeze through a standard office door and emerge in an upright position.

"Donde, if you broke this projector," screamed Springer jumping upward, "I hope the city takes it out of your pay check !"

"Kel, I'll help you set up," offered Donde.

"I don't need your help," spit Springer, "And the USB connector doesn't go in the power

UNDER THE BUS

socket."

"We would like to see the presentation some-time today," growled Alvin Phillips who had seen the film earlier.

The presentation was a video clip taken by the widow, Elizabeth Ghetti, and posted on social media. A copy of the clip was sent to Hobbs Creek mayor, the honorable Willard Green IV. A second copy filled a mini flashdrive and was now ready for viewing via Sergeant Kelsey Springer's mufti-functional projector.

"But, before we begin this presentation," said Phillips glaring at Juanito Lewis, "You need to know that Willard is already pressing me to ship your ass back to the big city."

"The Apple?"

"Yes, the Apple."

The presentation showed Juanito Lewis slipping through the shadows of Fosters Funeral Parlor, taking pictures of Elizabeth Ghetti who sat facing the casket that held Richard Ghetti. Occasionally, the midget would freeze in response to a door squeak or a pause in the organ music. At one point, Juanito actually snapped a picture of the widow from behind the casket.

"Sergeant, have you lost your senses," growled Phillips, "A viewing is sacred. A viewing is right next to the Holy Cow."

"The Holy Cow?" echoed Donde Clark, "Chief, *holy cow* is just an expression used by baseball fans nationwide and a well remembered commentator."

"Actually, *holy cow* is a oath or euphemism for "Holy Christ!" clarified Juanito Lewis, "The expression dates back to 1905 and maybe earlier."

"Could we get on with the presentation," cried Kelsey Springer.

Sometimes, life takes it's own little commercial breaks. This was one of those times. Springer's laptop froze up and while the eager projectionist rebooted, Juanito slipped a second flash drive into the USB port, and hit the center play arrow.

"And where did this film come from?"

UNDER THE BUS

asked Phillips as the leggy image of Elizabeth Ghetti flashed onto the screen.

"This is my side of the story," explained Juanito, "And you are not going to believe this shit."

"Juan, curb your tongue," said Donde.

"But Donde, there's a lotta shit, here."

"Curb your tongue!"

"Curbed."

Sgt Juanito Lewis had snapped multiple still shots of Elizabeth Ghetti, mixed with short video clips. One such clip began as Jeffery Hanson left the casket and sat down next to the widow. His head was down. Eventually, after some verbal exchange, her left hand found his right leg. Then, his right hand found her left leg.

"What the hell is going on?" queried Phillips.

"She's looking for his balls, Chief."

"Juan !" warned Donde.

"She's massaging his testicles," corrected the midget from New York City, "And it gets better."

Sergeant Lewis's next clip started and ended with business partner, Emerson Cook who had dropped into Hanson's vacated seat. The verbal exchange differed, but the hand play matched that of Jeffery Hanson.

"Damn!" cried Phillips, "She must be screwing both of them, but I thought Richard Ghetti had three partners."

"He does," verified Donde.

"So, where's the third partner?"

"He never showed up," replied Juanito.

The timetable for Richard Ghetti's viewing and funeral services had been well posted in all newspapers. and broadcast repeatedly by local radio and TV stations. Thus, Howard Dixon who was the banking firm's third partner, should have been there, and wasn't."

"I got some bad vibes about this," said Donde.

"Well, you two better get out there and find him," said Phillips motioning to Clark and Lewis.

UNDER THE BUS

"I thought we were off the case," said Donde.

"And who told you that?"

"Isabel."

"And what else did Isabel have to say?"

"She mentioned that your rug glue is running down your forehead," said Sergeant Springer.

Chapter 12

Howard Rutherford Dixon marched to the beat of his own bank roll. This third and missing partner envisioned rows of condos and low cost apartments, covering the two hundred acres that many Hobbs Creek residents still remember as Otto's Farm & Garden Mart.

There was a time in the nineteen fifties when the garden mart drew fruit and vegetable buyers from all corners of Lower Elk County. If you sought after firm, large, green grapes, you picked Otto's. If you hankered for Jersey corn or Jersey tomatoes, you drove to Otto's. Parking was free, and you could almost always hear the *chug chug* of a garden tractor off in the distance.

Otto Brown died in the mid-sixties and left his estate to Otto Brown Jr, who ran off to New York State in 1969 to join the then popular Wood stock movement. The younger Brown never

UNDER THE BUS

returned and sometime later the Hobbs Creek National Bank paid off the back taxes and seized the property for mortgage due. Millionaire and entrepreneur, John *The Baron* Kane was senior bank president at the time.

John ran the football for Mt Loyal High, and graduated valedictorian. His wide smile and rugged looks snagged Martha Grayson, home coming queen and daughter of the ailing Eli Grayson, who founded the Hobbs Creek National Bank. John's confidant manner kept the doors open through the Great Stampede, while a string of timely land deals branded him The Baron.

Ironically, John Kane's vision for Otto's matched that of Howard Dixon's – namely, apartments and low cost condominiums. Unfortunately for Kane, winds of change were already blowing. A new housing development named Wellington Woods had finished phase five and now had a civic club, turned political. These newcomers wore business suits, drove fast, and talked a lot about sand traps and wedge shots.

They also attended every township meeting to push a master plan for Hobbs Creek. Otto Brown's two hundred acre farmland would be part of that plan, but not for low cost housing or apartments. The newcomers envisioned bike trails, picnic areas and a possible retention pond to be named Browns Lake in honor of Otto Sr.

Some conflicts are destined to finish at the 38th Parallel, and the John Kane vs Wellington Woods was a case in point. Kane would not let go of the land, and the civic association managed to negate the rezoning needed to fit Kane's agenda - with the help of Mayor Willard J. Green.

Hobbs Creek ran as Mayor/Council govern-ment at the time, with Green as mayor and four councilmen named Wiley Brooks, Sam Burns, Joe Hicks and Harry Oberfest. The five men also doubled as the planning and zoning boards. Meetings were held in Green's basement while awaiting the new municipal building to open. City clerk, Becky Conners served as recording secretary and upon becoming pregnant, was replaced by a

UNDER THE BUS

slender township teacher, named Amy Wells, who became John Kane's water loo.

Amy was fresh from college and talked a lot about purpose in life and meaningful relationships. Her long legs could cause penis erection, and it was those legs that prompted Willard Green to hire Amy Wells as recording secretary. Green would almost salivate while watching Amy walk hither and yon, and he was peering out the casement window the night she left a meeting and climbed into a waiting car with John Kane.

"Damn!" cried Willard Green.

"What is it?" called down wife Edie.

"Nothin'," growled the mayor.

Sometimes, the word nothing can cover a whole soapbox opera of something. John Kane and Amy Wells had a history of slipping off together to share body juices. The indiscretions began two years back when John hired Amy to tutor the Kane's son Elmer, who suffered from a neuro-muscular disorder, commonly called Motor Slowness.

KYLE KEYES

Most Hobbs Creek residents thought Elmer to be retarded. He was not. The 305 lb youth had an average IQ. However, immaturity and blubber made Elmer the township dart board, which took a toll on his school grades. Martha Kane's answer to this dilemma was to dress Elmer in full suit and tie, if only to lumber down their long mansion driveway to get the mail. John Kane took another route. John hired the leggy Amy Wells to tutor Elmer through grade school graduation.

Often, John would drive Amy home on snowy nights. Small talk stayed strictly business and John kept his hands on the wheel, until one dark evening when the Call Of The Wild overcame virtue. One kiss led to another and they wound up parked behind the Hobbs Creek grade school, in the back seat of John's brand new El Dorado.

T'was a fantasy come true for John and Amy until Sergeant Jeeter Potts shone a flashlight through the rear window.

"I thought I recognized this car," exclaimed the deputy sheriff.

UNDER THE BUS

Clothes went back on rear fast. After which, John tried to buy off Potts with a hundred dollar bill, but to no avail. Eventually, gossip took it's toll, and the Kanes went on a second honeymoon to mend their broken marriage.

"So, maybe they need a third honey moon," said Willard Green reaching for the basement phone to call Martha Kane.

"Are we going on a honeymoon?" called down Edie Green.

"We're not going on a honey moon!" cried Green watching a file of black ants travel from the casement window, down the blond wall panel and onto the tile floor. Edie wore soda bottle lens for glasses, but could hear a beer can open from the far end of the house. He dropped the basement phone back onto the cradle and opted to go with Plan B. The zoning board met in two weeks, and John Kane's proposed endeavor required a majority vote to rezone the 200 acres from commercial to residential. Wiley Brooks and Sam Burns would vote yea. Joe Hicks and Harry

Oberfest would vote thumbs down, which would place Willard Green in the catbird seat.

When the hour of decision arrived, the meeting became one for the books. Mayor and council opted for secret voting, which required concealed ballots. No one knew how anybody else voted. John Kane kept calling for a recount. Amy Wells reminded John that the paper slips only numbered to five. The four councilmen stared at each other. John Kane glared at Willard Green who quickly gavel ed the proposed housing project to the back burner, until recent years when Howard Dixon pulled the right strings and managed to erect a row of apartment buildings on the east side of Route 92.

Time truly does heal all wounds, and current generations have new viewpoints. Newly weds and future home owners already filled the low rental apartments, while awaiting the condominiums and roof-mate homes, to be built on the west side. Otto's fruit stand was now a remodeled office building, and a new sign post read *Homes By*

UNDER THE BUS

Howard - a touch Dixon thought would temper the bitterness held by those residents who still preferred a park filled with trees, benches and bike trails.

Ironically, Dixon would never savor the finished version of *Homes By Howard.* Nor would he see the westside billboard that now reads *Future Home Of Hobbs Creek City Park*. Detective Sgt's Donde Clark and Juanito Lewis found the scrawny entrepreneur slumped in his swivel chair, staring at the traffic passing by the office picture window. Dried blood outlined a small hole in his forehead.

"He's dead?" screamed Alvin Phillips from the Hobbs Creek, station house.

"He a'int moving," said Donde.

"What do you need?" asked Phillips staring at the firehouse that sits at the corner of Elm and Main.

"Forensics and a body bag should do it."

"What happened?" queried Phillips.

"Somebody shot him," replied Donde.

KYLE KEYES

"That's it?"

"Well, he didn't commit suicide, Chief."

Phillips pivoted the swivel chair away from the parking lot window, and dropped the black phone onto the cradle. He clasped ten fingers behind his head and called out, "Isabel, get Juanito on the phone."

"He's not answering," came the reply..

"He never does," growled Phillips, "I thought maybe you'd get lucky. .. .get Donde on the phone."

"You just talked to Donde, suh."

"Isabel, get Donde on the horn!"

"Yes – suh."

Again, minutes later:

"This is Donde."

"Is Juanito there?"

"He is."

"Well, put him on."

"He's doing back flips," said Donde,

"Back flips?"

"Blood makes Juan nervous," explained

UNDER THE BUS

Donde, "And when Juan gets nervous he does back flips, and sometimes cartwheels."

"Cartwheels?"

"Cartwheels."

"Donde, I've had a bad day."

"Yes sir. .here's Juan."

"Juan, this is Chief Phillips. . .what's your take on this killing."

Juanito Lewis' forte was homicide, with circus acts coming in second. Phillips knew this. The Hobbs Creek police chief also knew that Juanito had an eye for detail and the logical mind required for cracking a murder mystery.

"So, what do we have, Sergeant Lewis?"

"This man was shot by someone he knew and trusted," said the midget detective.

"And how do we know that?"

"The phone es on the hook. We can check phone records, but it doesn't look like he tried to call out. Also, there's a loaded pistol here in the top drawer. . .untouched."

"A twenty-two?" asked Phillips, hopefully.

KYLE KEYES

"It's a thirty-eight, Chief," said Donde.

"What else, Juan?" asked Phillips.

"He was shot from the front," pointed out the midget detective, The killer had to circle the room and stand between the victim and the front window. So, it had to be someone he knew and trusted."

"And judging from the hole in the fore head," added Donde Clark, "The killer used a small caliber handgun and we all know who this points to."

*   *   *   *   *

Sometime later, ballistics confirmed that the gun used to kill Richard Ghetti was the same weapon used to kill Howard Dixon.

UNDER THE BUS

Chapter 13

Elizabeth Ghetti parked across the street from *Cookies Big Rig Towing* station. She killed the engine and lit a cigarette before joining the social media talk texting from her phone. *Likes* and *dislikes* continued to come in regarding her new hair style, which had went from below the shoulders to a short bobby cut, thanks to a clever placed wig. Thus far, her fans approved of this shorter look. She was also pleased that so many approved of her new blonde look, which would come in handy for the chore ahead.

She muted the phone and dropped a hand gun into her handbag. She exited the car thinking out loud, "People see what they expect to see. . . . . People don't recognize what they don't expect to see."

Humidity packed the late fall air as she crossed the street and walked boldly into the convenience store that sat behind a line of gas pumps. Distant thunder warned of a storm brewing. She looked around quickly and saw no one she knew. Relieved, she lit a cigarette and moved to the register.

"You're bucking the line," cried a silver haired lady in bib overalls.

"I'm just here to ask a question," said Elizabeth.

"And I just want a gas receipt," snapped the lady in bib overalls, "Damn pumps are always out of roll paper and you can tell Cookie I said that!"

Social Distancing was in effect, along with a local mandate to wear a face mask. Elizabeth Ghetti ignored the face mask ordinance because the cloth covering smeared her makeup. She cut through the long waiting line because she was in a hurry.

"Ma'am, we do require face covers to come in here," growled a pudgy cashier with a soiled hanker-chief wrapped around his stubby chin.

UNDER THE BUS

Elizabeth Ghetti pulled the revolver from her handbag and pointed the barrel at the cashier who slowly changed to a whiter shade of pale. Said Elizabeth, "Ok jelly belly, you can now remove your face mask so I can understand what you're saying . . .there . .isn't that a lot better . .I'll bet you can even breathe better . .Now for my question . . .I'm looking for Emerson."

"Emerson?"

"Mr Cook."

"Cookie's in the back garage working on one of the school buses," replied the cashier, weakly.

*   *   *   *   *

Emerson Cook's big rig towing service first saw the light of day as *Cookies Cities Service Garage And Gas Station,* back in the early nineteen fifties, when the gas wars were on. Emerson's grandfather, Jason Cook owned the original garage and put in two gas pumps to compete with Mayos Esso gas station, which lay directly across the highway. Cook opted for Cities Service, because the Oklahoma based company would sell fuel supplies to independent pump owners without an armload of restrictions. Jake was also a big fan of the Cities Service Concerts which aired on NBC until 1956, and would pipe the music outside for the enjoyment of his gas customers. Then, change pulled the rug out. Classical sounds gave way to Rock & Roll, and Old Man Mayo dropped his pump price to 13.9 cents a gallon to grab the shore bound motorists. Consequently, this one two punch flattened Jason Cook's garage and gasoline business until generations later when Emerson Cook graduated trade school.

    Emerson was born with a monkey wrench in his mouth – as they say. The pudgy, pimple-faced grandson of Jason Cook could fix a toaster, repair a grandfather clock, and reassemble an automatic transmission, blind-folded. The third generation Cook was also good at making a buck. In less than a year, he reopened the failed gas station, put in a dozen new pumps, added a convenience store, and

UNDER THE BUS

redesigned the garage area to hold township's dozen or so school buses.

Soon, township residents were bragging up Emerson Cook. His growing business and swelling assets prompted bank owner, Richard Ghetti to take on Emerson as a partner in the Hobbs Creek First National Bank and Trust.

Emerson's short comings could be wrapped up in one word – girls. When he was in grade school, he was the proverbial *ink well villain*. His teenage years included two *peeping tom* arrests. Once past puberty,, his vocabulary became a string of four letter words, and if a date would not submit, she had to walk home.. Consequently, his adult love life evolved into strictly *pay for sex.*

He lay now beneath a broken down, school bus as Elizabeth Ghetti called out his name. He dropped a greasy socket wrench and rolled out on the dolly saying, "Well, this is a fucking surprise, you've never brought your ass out here, before."

Not getting an answer, Emerson shielded his eyes from the sun and peered upward. Elizabeth

KYLE KEYES

Ghetti stood there with a gun barrel pointed downward. The blonde wig and jeans were new, but the demeanor and the voice were a dead giveaway.

"And what the fuck is this?" demanded Cook, "You know my lips are sealed."

The gunshot was the last sound Emerson Cook ever heard. One well placed bullet pierced his heart and it was lights out. He never felt Elizabeth Ghetti push the dolly back beneath the school bus. He never heard her mutter, "Your lips are sealed now for sure, and for your information, Emerson, you were a lousy piece of tail."

Minutes later, she drove off as the sound of silence gave way to the sound of distant sirens.

UNDER THE BUS

Chapter 14

Donde Clark and Juanito Lewis all but ran over Henry the gate guard, as the two Hobbs Creek lawmen crashed through the drop bar to the entrance of Lake Powhattan. Clark ignored the angry fist shaking in the rear view mirror, and held the pedal to the metal while Juanito Lewis had all lights flashing and sirens sounding When they reached Cabin 67 on the far side of the lake, Clark made a quick spin of the building and screeched to a halt at the front porch.

"Donde, you heet another railing."

"It's the builder's fault for putting these cabins in backwards," replied Clark, "These porches should be street side facing the road way, side walk."

"But there is no side walk."

"Exactly my point," explained Donde wiping clean his nickel and dime bifocals, "No sidewalk, no protective barrier. I really miss curbs."

"Donde, one more payroll cut and I won't have room and board money. You and April Jean will toss me under the trolley."

"I think you mean *under the bus* and not to worry," said Clark, "This is an active investigation and when an active accident happens during an active investigation, the department takes on the responsibility."

"Like when you ran over Wadsworth and the captain put it in the dead file."

"Juan, further investigation showed that the man was already dead under the snow."

"Donde, the further investigation came after we backed over the body, again."

Donde Clark erected the exit ladder so Juanito could climb down from the truck cab. Then Clark kicked his way through the front door and emerged with a shaken Jeffery Hanson, bath-robed and handcuffed.

"This will cost you your badge, officer," said the part owner of the Hobbs Creek bank, "I hope

UNDER THE BUS

you know that."

"Read him his rights, Juan."

\#   \#   \#   \#   \#

Later at police headquarters:

"The bull horn was my idea, Mr Hanson," said Police Chief, Alvin Phillips, "I wanted Mrs Ghetti to see us pick you up."

"Well, you succeeded," replied Hanson trying hard to keep his voice tone on an even keel, "I think everyone around the lake saw Mutt and Jeff here drag me away in handcuffs and I will be calling my lawyer."

"Understood and I do apologize," said Alvin Phillips, "However, I did have a purpose."

"What purpose?"

"That's police business."

"Police business?" screamed Hanson, "I'll tell you some police business, the first Miranda Right reads: *you have the right to remain silent –*

not – you have the fuckin' right to remain silent."

"I'll speak to Officer Lewis about his language," growled Phillips.

"And the second right is my right to an attorney, not my right to a fuckin' attorney."

"I'll talk to Sergeant Lewis," said Phillips, "And now I have something I want you to look at."

Forensic technician, Sergeant Springer had uploaded Juan's camera images onto the station house server, and had them ready for playback on a drop screen that covered the blank wall inside the interrogation room. An adjoining wall housed the entrance door, and the two remaining walls contained one-way-see-though, window glass for suspect identification. Phillips, Hanson, Clark and Lewis sat around a bare wood, table that filled the room center. Springer hit a play button on a remote control and seconds later, the air hissed out of Hanson.

The video clip was the one taken by Juanito Lewis at Richard Ghetti's viewing. Jeffery Hanson

UNDER THE BUS

sat next to Elizabeth Ghetti. All watching could plainly see the widow's left hand grab Hanson by the testicles. After which, Hanson's fingers slipped between the widow's legs, and worked their way up to her panties.

Hanson jumped to his feet. He pressed those same fingers through his wavy brown hair. He spun in a full circle, then muttered, "I can't talk about this."

"Mr. Hanson," ordered Phillips, "Sit down."

"But, I can't talk about this."

Alvin Phillips pushed the stop button on the film clip and opened a case file entitled Elizabeth Ghetti. He leafed through the newly printed pages and said, "Ms Ghetti is going to be charged with first degree murder. Mr Hanson, unless you cooperate you could be charged with accomplice to first degree murder."

The cornered book keeper stopped toying with a fatty cyst that grew beneath his hairline. His blue eyes jumped from stolid face to stolid face as he stammered to all, "We are having an affair . .Liz and I . .Corrrection. . were having an affair. I had no part in killing Richard."

"Sit down, Mr Hanson."

"You do know I'm a married man."

"This is a homicide investigation," said the Hobbs Creek top cop, "Sergeants Clark and Lewis are not from the vice squad."

Jeffery Hanson sat down slowly, and in tones even slower, recounted the intimacy that began at the Lake Powhattan Memorial Day picnic, and evolved into a series of skinny-dipping affairs after midnight.

"The center of the lake is a sandbar," said Hanson, "Our lake front cabins face each other and we would swim to that sandbar where the water is only waist high."

"Damn!" cried Juanito Lewis, "You were fuckin' her in the water."

"Juan," growled Alvin Phillips, "Isabel wants you out at the front desk."

"I don't hear Isabel calling me."

"Juanito, you have a phone call!"

UNDER THE BUS

"Yes sir."

Now, down to three people in the room, Alvin Phillips pushed the resume button on the video clip. Jumpy images showed Hanson leaving and Emerson Cook flopping into the vacated seat. There was no audio, but slow motion video frames followed Cook's fingers between Elizabeth Ghetti's legs, and up to her vagina.

"You don't seem very upset," noted Phillips.

"No reason to be," said Hanson, "Emerson was a former client of Elizabeth Ghetti. He probably thought he still had special privileges."

Chief Phillips and Sergeant Clark swapped quick looks after which, Phillips said, "We are listening."

"Before Elizabeth married Richard, she was a high ticket, call girl in a Mount Loyal City, gentleman's club. I don't know what a one night stand cost, but I've been told it was through the roof."

"And you got it for nothing?" asked Donde.

"I got it for nothing."

"And how was it?"

"It was through the roof."

Police Chief Phillips coughed loudly to break up the two way conversation between Jeffery Hanson and Donde Clark. Asked Phillips, "And Howard Dixon?"

"He was also a client of Elizabeth."

"Really?"

"Really."

"Well that's a real coincidence."

"Chief Phillips," said Jeffery Hanson taking a deep breath, "The whore house came first, not the bank. Ghetti, Cook and Dixon were three bachelors who happened to pay for sex with the same woman. The back yard details came to light later."

"And you weren't a client?"

"No, I met Elizabeth after she married Richard and moved to Lake Powhattan."

Alvin Phillips removed a set of paper documents from a cardboard folder. He fingered through the pages as he asked, "Do you own a gun?"

UNDER THE BUS

"No."

"We are looking for a twenty-two."

"I don't own a gun," repeated Hanson, "I had enough weaponry in the service."

"Army?"

"111 and 112," replied Jeffery referring to his MOS which was light weapons and heavy weapons, "If you fire that crap long enough, you go deaf."

"But you do know how to disassemble and assemble a handgun?"

"I do."

"And what are these receipts?" queried Phillips handing the documents to Hanson who studied the papers briefly and then explained they were the paper trail for money deposited in a Swiss bank account.

"The story is that you're skimming money from the bank and depositing it in this overseas account."

Jeffery Hanson grabbed the paperwork for a second look, then came close to laughing for the first time since the interrogation began.

"You find this funny?" asked Phillips.

"No, I find this absurd," replied Hanson shoving the files back at Phillips, "I do have a Swiss bank account, but this is not it. These spread sheets are part of the files I'm working on at home. I take work home occasionally."

"Well, the story is that Richard Ghetti stumbled onto this embezzlement, which is why he was killed."

"Embezzlement!" cried Hanson, "This account belongs to a client."

"I don't see a name," noted Phillips.

"But it does have an account number and that number will match a Jane or John Doe who wants to remain anonymous for whatever reason," explained Jeffery Hanson, "Now, let me ask you a question. Who came up with this embezzlement story and what are my files doing here?"

Alvin Phillips stuffed the scattered paper work back into the mailer, including Anita Hanson's goodbye note that called her husband *a no good,*

UNDER THE BUS

cheating, lying sack of shit. He spun the mailer around so Jeffery Hanson could read the return address and said, "It's been my experience that when a man cheats on his wife his wife usually knows about it, which brings up another question. . .just where is your wife? We haven't been able to locate her."

"She moved in with her sister," admitted the bank's bookkeeper, "Upstate. . .she won't be home, tomorrow. .or the day after . .or the day after. . .so what now . .am I being charged?"

"No charges," said Alvin Phillips staring hard at Jeffery Hanson, "But we are going to hold you overnight for your own safety . . .Howard Dixon and Emerson Cook were shot and killed earlier today."

Sudden silence.

Then, sudden silence became ear shattering. Hanson's head drooped. His fingers quivered. Phillips called for water and took that moment to beckon Donde outside the interrogation room. Said Phillips, "Put him in our downstairs holding cell, then round up Lewis and stake out Elizabeth Ghetti's place. If she so much as sneezes, I wanna know about it...and Donde?"

"Yeah, Chief?"

"What is it with Sgt Lewis and his mouth?"

"Juan is a midget living in a tall man's world," explained Donde, "Cursing is his way to push back. He grew up under the big top in his grandfather's carnival, and that's where he fit in. He left the circus to join reality, and all too soon, circus days faded like blacksmiths and pony express."

"And now he can't go home again," murmured Alvin Phillips.

"April Jean and I took him in when I was a Sgt Detective back in New York City. We never had kids, so he's it."

* * * * *

Minutes later, leaving the station house parking lot, Donde Clark braked long enough to slap a twenty dollar bill into Juanito's open palm,

UNDER THE BUS

Giggled the midget, "I knew she was fuckin' all four of them."

"And you were right," conceded Donde.

Chapter 15

Thanksgiving fell the next day. T'was not a happy Thursday for police dispatcher, Isabel Jackson, who slept through her snooze alarm before remembering that township agreed to pay double-time for the holiday. Then, in a rush to get dressed, she put on the bra with a bad snap, and the heels that rubbed a large corn on her big toe.

She walked now from parked car to ground floor elevator, favoring her left leg, no handbag, and phone to one ear. Her daughter Anabel was the proud mother of a 6 lb baby girl with blond hair and blue eyes, and Isabel who once believed that birds of a feather should stick together, now flew a banner that read: Pink Lives Matter. Suddenly, she turned from the open elevator and limped to the holding cells at the far end of the garage. She was halfway through burping procedures when she peered through the iron bars

UNDER THE BUS

to Cell One, dropped her cell phone and screamed.

Jeffery Hanson hung from the overhead ceiling fan. His feet dangled inches from the concrete floor. His head sagged sickly to one side.

Isabel screamed again, which brought the duty officer skipping down the inside stairwell, and soon, the stationhouse was alive with fire trucks, ambulances and police officers. A coroners report would later list the death officially as suicide from a broken neck that led to strangulation of the windpipe. Hanson had tied his bath robe rope around his neck, lassoed the overhead fan, and then jumped from a top bunk-bed. The fall force had pulled the fan's electrical box from the open raft ceiling, but failed to break loose the wired connections.

"I doubt if he suffered much," relayed the medical examiner to Anita Hanson, as she tore up the letter that referred to Jeffery as *a lying sack of shit,* "He probably blacked out instantly."

Chapter 16

Elizabeth Ghetti, Police Chief, Alvin Phillips and Detective Sergeant, Donde Clark sat around the bare wood, table inside the interrogation room. A wall clock read 3pm, which coincided with tiny chimes coming from the widow's cell phone. A 45 caliber handgun, and a 38 revolver lay next to her handbag. Asked Elizabeth, looking around, "Where's the midget?"

"Helping April with Thanksgiving Dinner," replied Donde crossing fingers and toes, "Juanito is a pretty good little cook. I'm only here because as you know, crime doesn't take a holiday."

"That's very clever," said Elizabeth, "Do you write your own material?"

"First off," broke in Chief Phillips looking at the widow, "I want to thank you for coming and bringing in these weapons. There are no pending charges here. This is just routine questioning."

"So, ask your questions."

"How long were you and Jeffery Hanson having this mid-lake rendezvous?"

Elizabeth Ghetti stopped posing for selfies and snapped closed her cell phone cover. She pushed her long hair back and over to cover the left shoulder and said, "I see Jeffery did some talking before he hung himself."

"He did mention that you had relations with all four owners of the Hobbs Creek National Bank."

"Sexual relations?"

"Yes – sexual relations," confirmed Phillips.

"They are the best kind don't you think?" said the very merry widow, "And just between the two of us, I too sneak a peek at computer porn – just now and then of course."

"You've been talking to Isabel I see."

"I have."

Flushing, Alvin Phillips moved to the door and hollered up the hallway, "We have a female suspect in here, and we need a female matron."

"Damn and double damn," said Elizabeth with a wry smile, "And I was hoping to get a peek under that toupee. Bald headed men just turn me on."

Phillips stayed in the open doorway until Isabel Brown Jackson showed up. The police chief whispered a few sentences to the police dispatcher, after which they took seats around the long interrogation table.

"Well," cried Isabel glaring at Elizabeth Ghetti, "I'll never confide anything to you again!"

"I didn't mean to rattle everyone's cage," said Elizabeth Ghetti.

"I'm not upset about being called *Old Chrome-Dome*," replied Phillips, "I'm angry about the *porn on the computer* accusations. Rumors like that could cost me my job."

"Chief Phillips," scoffed the widow, "We all sneak peeks at people doing it."

"I don't," chipped in Donde Clark.

"Really?" queried the widow.

UNDER THE BUS

"April Jean would kill me," said the seven foot detective sergeant, grabbing Phillips hair piece, that was now being sailed around the room. He handed the black wig to Phillips and muttered, "We need to get down to business, Chief."

Howard Dixon had been shot to death with a 22, sometime after 9am the day before. Shortly there after, Emerson Cook was gunned down while working under a school bus in his garage, not far away. The weapon used was also a twenty-two. Earlier, on this Thanksgiving Day, Jeffery Hanson who was the last of the bank owners, had apparently committed suicide, which left the Hobbs Creek National Bank in the hands of a receivership. Elizabeth Ghetti was the common link to all four men, which included her husband, Richard. Thus, all eyes were on this ex-call girl, turned wife and home maker.

"We need to know your whereabouts from 9am to noon, yesterday," asked Donde.

"Home, alone."

"Can anybody verify that?"

"No."

"No visitors?"

"No."

"How about your neighbor, Ms Chapman"

"Not at home all morning," said Elizabeth Ghetti, "And I would think that Jeffery Hanson is your logical suspect. He killed his partners out of jealousy, came down with the guilt's and then killed himself. Why don't you search his cabin for the murder weapon?"

"We've already done that," replied Donde, "And we have questioned Ivy Chapman. As it turns out, she was home all morning yesterday, and you won't."

"I see," said Elizabeth Ghetti lighting a cigarette while glaring at a no smoking sign, "Do I need to call my lawyer?"

"You are not under arrest," reminded Chief Alvin Phillips.

"I'm not?"

"No," said Alvin Phillips, "We don't have a motive for you. . . yet."

UNDER THE BUS

Elizabeth Ghetti gathered up her belongings and headed for the door. "When you get one, call me."

"We will," replied Phillips.

"And for it's worth," said the merry widow throwing Alvin Phillips a brazen wink, "You look more macho without the hair piece."

Isabel Brown Jackson was second to leave the room upon receiving a text that husband, Boa Beans Jackson would not be home for dinner. Chief Phillips and Donde Clark left last. They paused long enough to collect four peeping eyes stationed on the other side of the one-way window glass. Two eyes belonged to Leon Thompson, who cashiered at Cookie's Big Rig Towing Plaza. The second pair belonged to police sketch artist, Franco Lewandowski, who could make people come to life using chalk, pastels or oil brushes. The four men gathered in Phillips office, and waited for Donde Clark to bring in coffee and donuts.

"She doesn't bring coffee?" asked Thompson nodding toward the black woman seated at the desk just beyond the open doorway.

"We don't go there," grumbled Phillips, "Do we have an ID or not?"

Franco Lewandowski had did his best, and it was not easy with waving fists and Alvin Phillips toupee flying through the air. However, Franco did manage to sketch out a reasonable facsimile of Elizabeth Ghetti. After which, he changed the long dark locks to a cropped blonde wig, swapped the heels for keds, and covered the short skirt with a pair of tattled blue jeans.

"I don't know," said Thompson who had witnessed the arrival and departure of Elizabeth Ghetti on the day Emerson Cook was found dead under a school bus, "I don't remember the hair being that short . .make the hair longer. . .no that's too long . .

"Leon," growled Phillips, "Does that bike of yours still need a muffler?"

"I put on a glass pack."

"Well, a glass pack can be pretty noisy."

"Meaning what?"

UNDER THE BUS

"Meaning you could use a friend in the police department."

"Alvin, I needed a cop when this blond woman stuck that gun in my face and let's not forget who gives your boys a free sandwich at lunch time."

"She stuck a gun in your face?"

"I almost shit my pants."

"What kind of gun?"

" Alvin, I only saw the barrel."

"This blond woman?"

"Yes, the blond woman."

"Isabel, I need you in here to take a statement," called out Phillips.

No answer.

"Isabel!"

Still no answer. Then . .slowly . .ever so slowly, the door between Phillips office and the dispatch desk creaked open. The front strut to a three-legged walker showed first, followed by a pair of bright yellow handle grips, followed by Jeeter Potts.

KYLE KEYES

"Potts!" screamed Phillips, "What in the hell are you doing here!"

Jeeter Potts is now in his 80's, (at the time of this writing.) The retired desk sergeant for the Hobbs Creek station house is somewhat of a township icon, regarded by some as a law enforcement cornerstone, and maybe even a legend. Potts was on the force when Elmer Kane was killed, a murder mystery entitled The Pandarus File, that went unsolved from 1958 to post 911, when chief suspect Helena Hollister showed up in East Bank, Paris as Anna Ward. Jeeter also became the unwittingly pinocle partner of Olan Chapman aka The Vigilante, who remains at large, wanted for countless killings, deemed by many as justified because his victims were also killers.

However, the most repeated tales feature *Potts The Inventor,* and place Jeeter some where between Alexander Graham Bell and Thomas Edison. Jeeter never came up with a phone or light bulb but he did develop an electric car for the oil embargo days of the 70's. The car became a big hit

UNDER THE BUS

for drivers who kept an abundance of extension cords in the trunk.

Jeeter moved now with baby steps and stopped to the front of Phillips desk. Donde hustled a folding chair over to catch Jeeter as he collapsed downward to catch his breath.

"Potts, where the hell is Isabel!" cried Phillips.

"Give me a second, Chief," wheezed Jeeter.

"I like those yellow grips," said Donde staring at Jeeter's three wheel walker, now folded up.

There was an alternative purpose to the red rubber handle grips, repainted yellow. Often, Jeeter would stumble over a sidewalk crack, and the fluorescent grips gave first responders an easy spot.

"I''m waiting, Potts."

"Isabel ..had ..to ..run ..an ..errand."

"What kinda errand?"

"I couldn't catch all of it . . .something about the corner market."

"Potts, The Corner Market is only around the corner, and why didn't she summon a duty officer to man the desk?"

"Chief, this is Thanksgiving," replied the Hobbs Creek legend, "Everybody's home."

Minutes later, Donde Clark set Jeeter up with a cup of coffee, a chocolate donut and a laptop to take Leon Thompson's eyewitness statement, that Phillips thought, might lead to the apprehension of Elizabeth Ghetti. Then, hope became an ocean wave dashed against the rocks. Leon identified the blond on the sketch pad, as the blond who approached his cash register on the morning of the day his boss was found dead. Leon also ID'ed Elizabeth Ghetti as the brunette in the interrogation room. However, Leon refused to confirm that both images were the same person.

"Leon, I thought you said the blond woman was the same woman who stuck a gun in your face." said Police Chief Phillips.

"I said there are similarities."

"That's not what you said."

UNDER THE BUS

"Are you sure she couldn't see me on the other side of that window glass?"

"So, that's it," growled Phillips, "You are afraid of this skirt."

"Alvin, I came in here to identify a blond lady involved in a disturbance that happened over wearing a face mask at Cookies. Now, I find this woman might have gunned down three men in cold blood. So, what happens when she finds out I'm the guy who ID'ed her?"

"Leon, we will give you police protection."

Fear is a weapon in it's own right, and Thompson was not one to lead the cavalry into battle. He retied a loose face mask and left, picking up speed as he went. Jeeter left next to monitor the dispatch desk. Franco Lewandowski swapped shrugs with Phillips, checked his watch and muttered something that meant *you can't win 'em all*. Donde began wiping chocolate smears off the laptop keyboard when Isabel stormed in, clutching a grocery sack.

"Nice of you to come back," growled Alvin

Phillips.

"Would you believe they wouldn't take back this turkey," exclaimed Isabel, "And with all the business me and Beans give that store."

"Is that a turkey!" cried Donde, who had just received a text from wife April Jean that turkeys were sold out everywhere.

"This is a turkey," replied Isabel.

"You have a turkey?"

"This is a turkey," reaffirmed Isabel.

"Would you bring that turkey to my house for dinner?"

"You're inviting me for Thanksgiving ?"

"No, I'm inviting the turkey," replied Donde.

Isabel's face began to drop, then she caught that Donde Clark grin. The detective sergeant from the Big Apple owned a Broadway grin and two dimples that could make troubles melt and the world smile. She ran and jumped upward as Donde caught her in a roundhouse swing. Later, she text ed Boa Beans not to fret. She would not be eating alone. She was having Thanksgiving dinner with

UNDER THE BUS

two cops from New York City.

Chapter 17

"Olan, where are you ?"

"Portland."

"Portland!" exclaimed Ivy Chapman, "What the hell are you doing in Portland!"

"Helping out."

"Helping out who!"

"Ivy, you know me," replied Olan Chapman aka The Vigilante, "I only fight for Truth, Justice and the American Way."

"Olan, get your ass home."

"Trouble?"

"Big trouble," said wife Ivy, "Lizzie next door is blaming you for shooting her husband and two other owners of our bank."

"What!"

"Don't you read the papers?"

"Ivy, the only news we get is about Covid Nineteen."

UNDER THE BUS

"You're not funny, Olan."

"So, who did the shooting?"

"She did."

"So, have Phillips bring her in."

"He did."

"And?"

"He had to let her go," said Ivy Chapman, "She has no motive and no weapon."

"So how do you know she did it."

"Olan, am I ever wrong?."

"You're never wrong, Ivy . . .how's my rabbits?"

"The county keeps hauling them away, but they keep coming back."

"They're probably missing two."

"Olan?"

"I'm here."

"I need to talk to you."

"This sounds serious.'

"Olan, please listen."

"Listening."

"Olan . . .I'm seeing somebody."

"Oh. . ."

"Henry."

"Henry?"

"Henry Teasdale."

"Teasdale!. .the plumber? The guy with no bottom teeth and a hearing aid with a wire that runs down to his side pocket."

"Olan, he's a warm body and at least he's here and you're never gonna be here again. . .we both know that. . . .don't we. . Olan . . .Olan. . .. Olan?"

UNDER THE BUS

Chapter 18

Life's bad bounces can sometimes match those of basketball. A cheap shot can lead to a rebound that ends in a score for the visiting team. One week later, Olan Chapman showed up on skid row in Mt Loyal City, pulling his little red wagon, loaded with suitcases. He had no money, an empty belly, and needed a shave and haircut. He wore civies and packed no gun. America's number one fugitive also needed an empty tent.

Porkroll Annie was there to greet him. She came out of nowhere, leaped onto Olan Chapman's back, wrapped her jean covered legs around his waist and yelled, "Gotcha!"

"Annie ?"

"You came back!" cried the undisputed leader of the Lower Elk County homeless, who number 1,200, plus those not available for census. Half of that number live in and around Mt Loyal

City, in back alleys, vacant buildings, behind dumpsters. A good fifty vagrants stake down tents and lean-to's along Front Street, which divides city buildings from South Branch Creek.

Olan had peeked into the first tent and caught a black skillet on the nose. The second tent brought screams from two runaways, making a study of the birds and bees. The third tent was empty. Thus, Annie set up housekeeping for Olan in this waterside adobe, vacated by a hobo who had failed to fit in with the *In Crowd*.

Annie and Mount Loyal Police Chief, Frank Cantene co-existed with ground rules set up by Cantene and enforced by Annie: there was to be no street fighting, shoplifting, excessive noise after dark; no heavy pot smoking and no sidewalk demonstrations. Now and then, Cantene would show up with bullhorn and remind everyone to take their pot to Portland, and their belly-aching to Pennsylvania Avenue.

"I don't have any pot," smiled Olan, who was against smoking before it was fashionable to

UNDER THE BUS

be against smoking.

"Have you had dinner?"

"I could go for a good steak."

"How 'bout hotdogs and beans."

"I love hotdogs and beans," cried Olan, again toting Annie on his back, and squirming as she tickled his rib cage.

"Then, tote me to my tent."

"Yes, your highness."

Olan Chapman and Porkroll Annie met a couple years back when Chapman showed up on skid row as Calvin Cooper, an 18th Century cavalry soldier who died at The Alamo on March 6, 1836. Cooper, nicknamed Cannonball, was the third alter-ego for Olan Chapman aka The Vigilante, who had previously morphed into a forest ranger named Jesse Joe Jacks, and a deputy marshal named Samuel Leroy McCoy from 1876 Dodge City.

Dr Adler Dearwood, the Buffalo City psychiatrist, believed that Chapman's strange metamorphose was triggered when the meek computer wizard would don the outfit of someone he once was in another life cycle. Dearwood believed that the subconscious brain can cause a change in our physical properties, more so than the conscious brain.

"Well, your *change of character* thing saved my bacon," said Annie dumping canned beans into a cooking pot, "Those two thugs came close to making it lights out."

The two thugs were money collectors for a city loan shark with a long reach and short temper. Their target was a hobo named Bobby who lived two tents down from Annie. At the time, Bobby's brother Jerry was there, trying to convince Bobby to give up his wandering ways, and return home to his wife and kids.

"I was surprised you pointed out Bobby's tent," remembered Olan.

"I had a brain cramp," said Annie.

Minutes later, the two strangers dragged Bobby and Jerry from the tent, and began pistol whipping the two brothers. Screams filled the night air. Tent flaps opened to let startled eyes peek out. Annie ran out to squash the fighting,

UNDER THE BUS

only to get thrown to the ground, and take a vicious kick to the ribs.

"Maybe we need to make an example out of these two, Moe."

"Good idea, Manny. These hobo's need to see what happens when they welch on a loan. Why don't we flip for the honors."

No one saw Olan fade from the scene.

Everyone saw Calvin Cooper arrive.

The Cavalryman from yesterday showed up with a powder pistol, and a Bowie knife on each hip. After a brief confrontation, one blade pierced the heavier stranger in the stomach, The second knife made another air duct in the second man's throat.

The two men fell to the ground.

Annie screamed.

Cooper disappeared.

"They would have popped us for sure if this Cannonball guy had not showed up," said Annie, "All three of us. .bastards. .I never came that close to dying in my life."

"And they were looking for jack?"

"Which was a waste of time," replied Annie, "Bobby had no money and Jerry just about made ends meet with his meals on wheels business."

Gerald Zeltz would die a short time later in a drowning accident. After which, Robert "Bobby" Zeltz left skid row to take over Jerry's *meals to homeless* business, plus other good Samaritan chores performed by his deceased brother.

"No evil deed goes unrewarded," smiled Annie, "So what brings you back here?"

Olan Chapman poured more coffee into his cup and Annie's cup, pushed aside a bowl of beans, and waved a slice of bread, asking, "You got any butter?"

"Real butter?"

"Yes, real butter."

"Olan!" laughed Annie, "Whatdaya think this is, the Waldorf?"

The two squeezed through the tent flap and emerged into the chilly night air. Mount Loyal, N.J. grew from farmland back in Civil War days. The city was patterned after many southern towns where main structures circle a central park. Olan pointed across Mt Loyal's, Patriot Park to rooftops that ran along the distant skyline. Said Olan, "One of those buildings hold the law offices of Dunn, Piddle and Pawnitt, whose motto is: *We don't dawdle, we're on it.*"

"So you need a lawyer," grinned Annie reaching for Olan's hand, "Of course. America's Most Wanted man could always use a good lawyer."

"Annie, this is serious."

"Okay, this is serious."

"I need to get into the firm's office," said Olan, "I'm being accused of three killings I didn't do, and the papers I need to clear my name are in their third floor safe."

"You are sure of this?"

"I googled it."

"Of course," smiled Annie as they walked along South Branch Creek hand in hand. Crickets began to take over the night air, and a sudden bullfrog blast caused Annie to squeeze Olan's fingertips a bit more tightly. They stopped in front of a long line of aluminum sheds, connected to the city's water supply.

"Well, these are new," noted Olan.

"Showers," explained Annie, "The mayor gave in on trying to relocate the homeless, and did a 180% turnabout. Morrison said if you can't move 'em out, at least clean 'em up."

"Is this a Saturday Nite Special?" laughed Olan.

"This is any night special," replied Annie, then without warning, the self appointed leader of skid row dropped the bomb, "Olan, I know about your wife and Hank Teasdale."

Olan dropped Annie's hand.

A long silence followed as the two locked eyes: Annie waiting for some type of an explosion; while Olan mentally fished through canned stories of *who said what* and *who did what*. Then, staring at the rooftops that were his destination, he blurted out, "This is not Ivy's fault. She needs a man in her life and I can't go home again. Maybe never. . .so . .how did you find out about Teasdale?"

Annie laughed. Not a belly laugh, but a *break the tension* laugh. She retook Olan's hand and said, "You have a million dollar price tag on your head. You should be nicknamed Front Page News. Ivy is front page news, also. The two of you belong on the tabloids.

"So, what now?" queried Olan.

Porkroll Annie swung Olan's gaze off the distant buildings and back onto her, saying, "Here's our plan, blue eyes. The night belongs to us. When you finish running across rooftops, and breaking into safes, you get your ass back here to these showers. And you need a shave. Then, you report to my tent."

Olan Chapman aka The Vigilante grabbed Annie by the other hand and made a small swaying motion., like two teenagers in love. He peered over an oval face that owned two sensuous lips and asked, "Is the hair bun staying up or coming down, Annie?"

KYLE KEYES

"The hair bun is coming down, Olan."

UNDER THE BUS

Chapter 19

Sgt Donde Clark raced between a double row of black and white squad cars, and screeched to a stop on the ground floor of the Hobbs Creek Police Station. The sudden jolt threw his mini partner into the windshield.

"This just in!" cried the detective sergeant double checking a phone text, "The chief's got some thing really big!"

"Really big?" asked Juanito.

"Big like in huge!" exclaimed Donde.

The two men scampered up the rear steps of the station house and paused at the dispatch desk. Isabel Jackson kept her face down while she pounded on the glass overlay, smeared with coffee stains. The two men shrugged and burst into Chief Alvin Phillips' office.

"This is big," said township's top cop tossing a manilla folder toward Donde, "This is real big."

"Big like in elephant?" asked Juanito

"Maybe bigger," replied Phillips.

Donde Clark leafed through typewritten pages and suddenly exclaimed, *holy cow!* He handed the paperwork to Juanito Lewis who responded with, "holy shit ! Does this mean forty million dollars!"

"It doesn't mean tootsie rolls," said the police chief blowing smoke toward the ceiling fan, "Now we got ourselves a motive."

Richard Ghetti Sr had left Richard Ghetti Jr forty million dollars in a last will and testament, just before the elder Ghetti passed on. The will would be executed upon Richard Jr's 40th birthday, with four stipulations. Young Ricky would have to be married, clean shaven, give up race car driving and lose the rap-crap music.

"Sounds like my father bringing down the big hammer," said Juanito doing a cartwheel over a magazine rack loaded with food recipes.

"Where did this come from, Chief?" asked

UNDER THE BUS

Sgt Donde Clark referring to the Ghetti last testament and will.

Phillips pressed an intercom button and called for Sgt Springer and the stationhouse video cart to come front and center. Said Phillips, "Kel, you want to run that video clip, again."

"Which one, Chief?"

"The one we took off our security camera."

"Chief, you've already looked at that twice."

"I want Sgts Clark and Lewis to see it."

The film footage came from the security camera focused on the dispatch desk. The date was current. The time was 8:20am, twenty minutes after the daytime shift came on. A man approached the desk and handed Isabel Jackson the file folder that contained the Ghetti last will and testament. He was medium height, clean shaven, but dressed like a hobo.

"I must be be missing something, Chief," said Donde, "Are we supposed to know who this is?"

"Springer, blow it up a little," said Phillips,

"Ok, stop. . .recognize him, now?"

"No."

"Springer, use your *image magic* to remove the face mask."

"Holy cow," cried Donde a few seconds later, "It's the guy on the wanted posters."

"Holy shit," echoed Juanito, "It's Chapman!"

"Olan Chapman," confirmed Phillips, "Right here in our building. Just walked in brazen as can be, handed Isabel the file folder, and walked out."

"Wow!" exclaimed Donde, "And that cool, one million dollar reward walked out with him. . .no wonder Isabel is pounding on the desk top. . .so how did Olan Chapman come by this folder?"

Alvin Phillips took a local call from a woman who wished to report a man entering the bank, with no face mask. The rotund police chief stared at the ceiling fan, muttered *heaven help us*, took a coffee sip, burped, patted his belly and returned his attention to Donde Clark. Said Phillips, "Olan Chapman is classified as paranormal, for reasons beyond my comprehension. He can become some

UNDER THE BUS

one he once was. One of those alter- ego's is a second story man, nick-named *Silhouette*. I got word earlier from Mt. Loyal Police that person or persons unknown had broken into the law firm of Dunn Piddle & Pawnitt. They found the safe open, but could not be sure if anything was missing until Ghetti's will showed up here."

"So now we can pickup Elizabeth Ghetti?"

"Not so fast, Donde," said Phillips taking his window perch overlooking the parking lot, "I've also been on the phone with Lee Galleger from the State Attorney's office. He wants the weapon."

"But Chief, we have opportunity and now we have motive."

"But we don't have means," said Phillips, "This case will be Elizabeth Ghetti versus the state of N.J. And Galleger wants the murder weapon."

Juanito Lewis finished a series of back over flips, and came to a sitting position on a Chinese throw rug in front of the police chief's desk. He jumped up quickly and said, "We never searched her car."

"You never searched her car?" said Phillips.

"We never searched her car," echoed Donde Clark, "We searched her cabin, we searched the area around her cabin. But, we never searched her car."

Alvin Phillips left the window perch and flopped into the cushy swivel chair that hissed like a female cobra, guarding a nest of babies. He picked up a phone to secure a proper warrant, then decided to run the operation covert for fear of tipping his hand. He dropped the handset back onto the black receiver and stared at the two NYC detectives, saying, "No lights and sirens going through the gate. No bells and no whistles at bikini clad bodies. I don't want one call from a Powhattan Lake resident claiming there's police disturbance of any kind. Again, this operation is going strictly undercover."

"You got it Chief," said Donde Clark.

"You got it Chief," said Juanito Lewis.

UNDER THE BUS

Chapter 20

Donde Clark swung his monster-wheel pickup into Cabin 18 and braked over the plank risers that led up to the front porch. Sounds of wood splitting came from beneath the front axle.

"Oh shit," cried Juanito.

"I still can't get used to these tri-focals," said Donde Clark wiping off the brown horn-rims.

Seconds later, Ivy Chapman burst out the front door, shotgun in hand, her heavy eyebrows furrowed in anger. Her black forearm hair seemed to bristle as she fired the first barrel, a wild shot that went high over the truck's windshield. The second buckshot load went under the vehicle.

"Damn," cried Juanito seeking cover beneath the dashboard.

"Oh shit," exclaimed Donde rolling out the driver's door, "Mrs Chapman! It's us, Don and Juan."

KYLE KEYES

"I just had these porch steps repaired from a mail truck visit!" screamed Ivy, "Look at this railing! Busted again! And my steps, smashed! How do you kids today learn to drive, playing bumper cars!"

Donde managed to slip out of his tee shirt and use the under garment as a white flag. Recent rain had turned much of the ground to mud, and he rolled to a sitting position as Ivy stuffed a fresh cartridge into the shotgun. Said Donde wiping hands off on jeans, "Mrs Chapman, let me remind you we are police officers."

Slowly, Ivy lowered the weapon to say, "Olan is not here, officers. Read my lips. Olan Chapman is not here!"

"We are not looking for your husband."

"Who are you looking for?"

"Can we come in?"

Another long pause.

"Ma'am?"

"You can come in," said Ivy looking at Donde, "The midget stays outside."

UNDER THE BUS

"He's not wearing his spurs."

"He stays on the porch!"

"Yes ma'am."

"And I don't want him knocking over my bird feeder doing cartwheels !"

"Yes ma'am."

The kitchen window to Cabin 18 faced the stony driveway to Cabin 20. Donde Clark pulled a data sheet from a vest pocket, and checked description details with the red SUV that sat in the driveway. Said Donde, "I can't see the tag number, but I would guess the vehicle belongs to Ms Elizabeth Ghetti."

"I could have told you that," replied Ivy, "You only needed to ask."

"Just following police procedure, ma'am."

"Well, her car's not for sale," said Ivy.

"We don't want to buy her car," replied Donde, "We need to search her car."

"Well, you could have did that outside, instead of running down my porch railings," said Ivy.

"Couldn't do that," explained Donde, "We don't have a warrant."

"You two don't seem to have a warrant for anything," said Ivy, "Would you mind telling me what this is all about."

The two homicide detectives from New York City needed to search the vehicle for the missing 22 caliber pistol, but they wished to do so unbeknownst to their prime suspect. Sergeant Clark believed that since the two neighbors were somewhat intimate, that Ivy Chapman might be helpful.

"We Goya's are always ready to help out the authorities," said Ivy Goya Chapman, "My roots are in San Juan, Puerto Rico, but I do have cousins right here in the states."

"I have cousins here in the states," cried Donde.

"So, it really is a small world after all," said Ivy.

"And getting smaller all the time," said Donde putting on his best smile.

"She frequently goes to Sallys Beauty Salon out on the highway," said Ivy eventually joining

UNDER THE BUS

Donde at the window, "Hair, nails, pedicure, facial. She's inside for hours."

"Thank you, ma'am."

"Just don't tell Lizzie that I ratted her out," said Ivy, "We're currently not on speaking terms and she does take me shopping . . .when she's not pissed off at me."

"Scout's honor," promised Donde

"And officer?"

"Yes, Ma'am?"

"You can tell Chief Phillips that township will be getting billed for my porch steps and railing!"

"Yes, Ma'am."

Chapter 21

Sally's sat in a strip mall on State Route 91, just east of Hobbs Creek. The busy salon was flanked by a cell phone outlet and a popular chop shop that would cut the steak of your choice, your way. Donde pulled into the meat market and braked to the blind side of Sally's.. The red SUV was parked facing the salon's giant picture window.

"Damn," said Donde.

"Damn," echoed Juanito.

"So, how do we get into the van without being seen?"

"The rear door," replied Juanito.

"You sure?"

"There's a key lock in the rear handle."

"You sure?"

"I know what I saw," replied the midget," You got the magic key?"

"I got the magic key," said Donde, "You

UNDER THE BUS

got the magic fingers?"

"Does a bear piss in the woods. "

"You're all class," responded Donde as the two law officers from New York City, exited the pickup truck and hit the ground, belly down. The parking spots from the meat market to the beauty salon changed from tar to rough gravel, and soon Donde had a load of loose stones up his under shorts. Said the seven foot tall cop, "You better be right about that door handle."

"I know what I saw," whispered the midget crawling knee high over the abrasive pebbles, "And it's not much farther. We are almost there."

Sallys consisted of four departments for self appearance: hair dressing; manicures; pedicures and facials. The Widow Ghetti lay in a window stall having her toenails clipped and painted. Neither man saw the beautician peering between the window curtains.

"I didn't think the purple nails would fly," said Sally who kept the better tippers for herself.

KYLE KEYES

"It was my fans," purred Elizabeth, "Almost to the man they wanted me to change my nails back to pink and you know what a problem it is to go from a dark shade back to a lighter shade.."

"Well, it looks like two of those men are now crawling toward your car," said the skinny proprietor with a beak for a nose and an eagle eye, "Should I call the police?"

Elizabeth Ghetti swung upward from the leather cot and joined Sally at the window in time to see Donde and Juanito disappear behind her red SUV. She sighed and said, "Sally, they are the police."

"Really?"

"Really."

"They look like a Vaudeville show."

Juanito Lewis had the magic key inserted in the SUV's rear door handle when a key ring fell from above. Muttered the midget staring up a long pair of female legs, "Don't shoot."

"I'm not armed," said the widow.

UNDER THE BUS

"That's good," said Donde Clark who failed to see Elizabeth Ghetti arrive in time to warn his partner, "We can explain this."

"Try the key that came with the vehicle," said the widow, "It might work easier."

"Ma'am, we really can explain this," said Donde.

"Save your lies," replied Elizabeth Ghetti, "We all know you are looking for a 22 caliber pistol. So, search away. If you find anything, I'll be inside getting my nails finished."

Moments later, police cars rolled in from all directions.

"Damn, I knew she was going to call the cops," said Donde.

Chapter 22

Police Chief, Alvin Phillips stood at his second story, office window and stared down at the black and whites that dotted the police headquarters, parking lot. An ambulance and ladder truck blew their way out of the firehouse across the busy intersection of Elm and Main. The seventh edition of a springer spaniel named Bingo, paused to pee on a nearby fire hydrant. Phillips swore softly and turned abruptly to mutter, "You guys knew we were flying by the seat of our pants on this one."

"Chief, there was no one in sight," murmured Donde staring at a coffee stain on the hardwood floor, "We thought we could go undetected."

"Sergeant, you are seven foot tall," growled the Hobbs Creek top cop, "When you are on your knees, you are higher than a camel."

UNDER THE BUS

"Chief, she has to have that 22 somewhere."

"Was it in her car?"

"No, Sir."

"Did you find it in her cabin?"

"No, Sir."

"Maybe she has it in her panties," chipped in Juanito Lewis.

"Funny man," said Phillips, "And Juan I want you to stop doing back-over flips and sit down. We are in some deep shit, here."

"I don't think we can get a warrant to search the lady's panties," called in Isabel from the dispatch desk.

Alvin Phillips took a routine phone call, closed the door that divided his office from the switchboard, and walked back to the window that overlooked Elm and Main. All was now quiet below. Said Phillips, "This lady knows the right people in the right places. So far, I've gotten a call from the mayor, internal affairs, the press, and Judge Lampi who rode in the same golf cart with the deceased Richard Ghetti. They want the case dropped."

KYLE KEYES

"Chief, this lady murdered her husband," said Donde Clark looking up from his shoelaces, "And, she also killed two of his business partners."

Alvin Phillips frowned. He straightened his itchy hair piece which always seem to slip when he became cornered. He didn't like fighting with Mayor Green, and Judge Lampi had already warned him straight out to leave the widow alone, without solid evidence to tie her to the shootings. He lowered the open window and turned to inform the two detectives from New York City that he was closing the case, which brought Donde Clark to his feet.

"Chief, if we drop this case, the lady gets away with first degree murder!"

"Sergeant, as of now, this lady has gotten away with first degree murder – so be it."

"Chief, let me remind you," said Donde, "We are two of New York City's finest."

"Meaning?"

"Surveillance is our middle name," replied the Big Apple detective, "We have techniques not

UNDER THE BUS

found in the officer training handbook."

Alvin Phillips returned to the parking lot window, raised the bottom sash to better see town hall, grunted, dropped the bottom sash and returned to his desk to grumble, "If you guys cost me my job, you will be back on your way to New York City."

Chapter 23

Fate can be fickle, fate can be fun, but it does happen while we look the other way. Don and Juan spent the next week tailing Elizabeth Ghetti, on the slim chance she might lead them to the missing 22 caliber pistol, when Hank Teasdale showed up at police headquarters.

"Alvin is on the phone," said Isabel, "Have a seat and try not to get too much mud on the floor."

"Yes, ma'am."

"Does Missus Chapman allow you to wear those boots in the house?"

"No ma'am."

"Then, why are you wearing them in here?"

Hank Teasdale dressed daily in clean work jeans, but like many local plumbers, his rubber boots were mud caked from working on septic systems. Mt Loyal, Carson City and Hobbs Creek all

UNDER THE BUS

had city sewerage, but outlying areas still relied on leach fields and waste tanks that ran on float systems emerged in urine. Crowed Teasdale from time to time, "At least computers will never replace toilets and that's a good thing."

"So what brings you to police head quarters?" asked Phillips hanging up from his phone call.

"Alvin, tell that plumber I'm putting his boots under the water hose!" called in Isabel, "There's no excuse for boots this muddy."

"I was out at McGreger's old place," explained Teasdale, "They got one of those three float systems and one pump wasn't coming on, so of course I had to go down in the hole."

"Muddy boots should be the apex of our problems," grumbled Phillips, "Can we cut to the chase here,"

Hank Teasdale reached deep into a side pocket, pulled out a cartridge holder and slapped the metal magazine onto Phillip's desk, saying, "This takes twenty two caliber bullets."

"You found that in McGregers septic tank?"

"No, I found that when I got back to Ivy's. .. you know I pay room and board at the Chapman residence."

"Hank, the whole town knows you're sleeping with The Vigilante's wife."

"Anyway, I just pulled into the driveway when the lady next door beckoned to me," continued the plumber, "She had a stopped up toilet she wanted me to look at."

Suddenly, Donde Clark jumped from the lumpy office sofa and crossed the room to join Hank Teasdale in front of Chief Phillips desk. Clark grabbed the metal holder and cried something that sounded like *holy cow*. The magazine was built to hold nine shells, not six.

"Is that significant?" asked Phillips.

"I think we better get Springer in here," replied Clark.

Moments later, Sgt Kelsey Springer showed up carrying a fully assembled 45 cal handgun. Springer wasn't the greatest shot in the world, but this head of ballistics was adept at assembling and

UNDER THE BUS

disassembling weapons of all makes and calibers. Said Springer, "As you can see, when I pull the stock magazine from the 45, this nine shell 22 holder slips right up here."

"Damn, that's how she did it," exclaimed Alvin Phillips, "She used a calibration convertor ! "

"Not so fast," cautioned Springer pulling off the top half of the forty-five, "You need the proper slide to line up the cartridges with the barrel."

Phillips swung his attention to Teasdale. "You found this magazine in Elizabeth Ghetti's toilet?"

"Is that the lady who lives in Cabin 20?"

"It is."

"I found it in the trap to the toilet."

"What about the slide?"

"I don't know anything about a slide."

"Chief, the slide would be too big to flush down a toilet," said Donde Clark.

Alvin Phillips raised from his plush swivel chair with a slight back groan and returned to the parking lot window where he did his best thinking.

Eventually, he turned to ask, "Will the barrel from the slide fit into the forty-five?"

"Yes it will," responded Springer.

"So, you can fire the weapon with no slide."

"Yes, but you would have to load the shells one at a time."

"And that would line up with something that Ivy Chapman said," recalled Donde, "Ms Chapman said there was a pause between gunshots, almost as though the shooter enjoyed watching the victim die."

"And what do you think, Juan?" asked Phillips.

The midget stopped spinning on a nearby saddle chair and grabbed the cartridge holder to command center stage attention. "To buy this part, the shooter had to purchase the entire conversion kit. If the shooter purchased the entire conversion kit, the shooter would use the whole conversion kit."

"I have to agree with Juan," said Phillips after another long look out the window, "Hence, we will go on the assumption that there's a slide out there somewhere. If we can find that slide, we can

UNDER THE BUS

blow the high and the mighty off their cat bird seats."

Chapter 24

Henry the gate keeper waved a dozen residents through the park guest entrance, and then left the Lake Powhattan guard house to greet the shiny black pickup with the monster wheels and the dice cubes that hung from the rear view mirror. He waited for the last angry horn to silence, before swapping hand waves with Sgt's Donde Clark and Juanito Lewis.

"What's wrong with the pass through gate?" asked Donde.

"Electric eye's busted," grumbled the gate man, "Last week a motorist drove through it, and a month ago the lift motor broke which happens when our snow bird residents don't appropriate enough funds to keep up maintenance repairs."

"Is Ms Ghetti home?"

"Ms Ghetti left to get her nails done."

UNDER THE BUS

"Henry, Ms Ghetti just had her nails done."

"That was her toe nails," said the keeper of the gate, "Today, she gets her finger-nails done."

"Interesting," mused Donde Clark, "And she confides all of this to you?"

"She confides this to her neighbor Ivy, who lives with my brother Hank, who checks on me daily because I suffer from an affliction known as congestive heart failure."

"Holy smoke," cried Donde smacking his forehead, "You are brothers. Juan here has been saying all along that you two look like each other."

"Twins."

"And you are both named Henry?"

"No, I'm Henry and Hank is Hank," said the gate keeper, "We were named after our birth father whose name was Henry Hanks."

"So, who is Teasdale?" queried Donde.

"Our stepfather."

"I'll tell you what, Henry," said Donde pulling a wad of bills from his wallet, "Up in the Big Apple, we pay informants for information. But in this case, how about we slip you some money not to spill the beans."

"Spill the beans about what?"

"We need to snoop through the Ghetti cabin and we don't have a warrant," admitted Donde.

Henry Hanks Teasdale backed away from Sgt Clark and the money, saying, "With all due respect, officer, this is Hobbs Creek, not New York City. I would not feel right taking your money. However, you can trust me not to say anything."

"Thank you, Henry," said Donde, "I'll join you back here in a moment."

Breaking into Elizabeth Ghetti's cabin would prove easier than breaking out. The two lawmen opted to use a rear window to avoid detection. Donde Clark jimmied the swivel latch and then hoisted Juanito Lewis through the opening. After which, Clark returned to the gate house for lookout duty. Thirty minutes later, Lewis found the slide. The widow had hidden the top part of the conversion kit under the sub floor at the bottom of

UNDER THE BUS

the sink.

Then the unexpected happened.

Instead of calling Donde, Juanito elected to jump from the window ledge to the ground. It would have been an easy feat for the ex-circus acrobat, but his boot spur hung up on the window ledge and the body jolt that followed, brought down the window.

Detective Sergeant, Juanito Lewis now hung helplessly, upside down.

His cell phone lay on the cobblestone drive way, just out of reach.

"What are you doing, mister?" asked a small voice wearing blue sneakers with pink shoelaces.

"Kid, hand me that phone," said Juanito.

"I can't."

"You can't!. .why?"

"I'm not allowed to talk to strangers."

"I'm not a stranger, I'm a police officer."

"You don't look like a police officer."

"I'm working undercover," said Juanito, "Now, hand me the phone."

KYLE KEYES

"I can't."

"But the phone is right there."

"I'm not allowed to talk to strangers."

"You don't have to talk to me," gasped Juanito, "Just push the fucking phone over here."

"I don't think I like you," said pink shoelaces.

"You don't like me!" cried Juanito, "You don't even know me."

"I'm going home and get my father."

"Oh shit," muttered Juanito.

Moments later, Horace Horatio showed up with fifty neighbors who constituted Lake Powhattan's CFA (Citizens For Action). Horatio was now president of this civic association, a position he inherited when former president, Maryann Grundy suddenly packed up and moved to San Diego to live with her twin sister. Over the years, the antsy Maryann had swapped lakeside cabins three times, so it came as no surprise when she moved out altogether and left her first lieutenant, Horace Horatio in charge - a move that made Horace happier than a hog in slop. He raised a black and

UNDER THE BUS

yellow bull horn to lips and bellowed, "YOU . ..LEANING AGAINST THE BUILDING . .COME . . OVER HERE ! AND DON'T TRY TO RUN, THE PROPER AUTHORITIES HAVE BEEN CALLED! "

  * * * * *

  Three hours later, Detective Sergeants Clark and Lewis were placed on administrative leave pending a hearing by Internal Affairs and the N.J. State Attorneys Office.

  "Chief, you really threw us under the bus on this one," argued Donde, "You knew we didn't have a warrant."

  "Donde, that slide you and Juan brought back, had no barrel. It was hollow. Nothing inside. And without a barrel, there is no ballistic report. Nothing to prove that Mrs Ghetti killed anyone."

  "So the end does justify the means," replied the sergeant detective from New York City, "Even here in Hobbs Creek."

  A silent pause followed. After which, Alvin Phillips said, "Donde, it wasn't so much the warrant business. I'll have you two back to work within 48 hours. What really pissed everyone off was Sgt Lewis offering a little boy a piece of candy."

UNDER THE BUS

Chapter 25

Alexis Grumman Wade left the parking lot and walked up the long flight of marble steps that led to the Federal Intelligence Center, located in Warrenton, VA. The morning air was clear and crisp which amplified the diesel horns coming off the Eastern By Pass. Stanley the security guard waited at the top of the steps.

"I need to see your ID."

"You want an ID, Stanley? How 'bout a knuckle sandwich."

"Thank you, but I brown-bag my lunch."

"Stanley!. .get some fresh batteries for your goddam hearing aid."

Alexis Grumman was among the first United States women to earn the rank of Lieutenant General in the armed forces. The three star, single mother served tours in Korea, Germany and Vietnam. She wore the Legion Of Merit, and two Meritorious Service medals on her smart uniform jacket. She served much of her military career coordinating intelligence with remote field operations, where she had a reputation for walking through land mines, and spitting on rattlesnakes. Now, she heads up the Department For Paranormal Affairs, a small federal agency that investigates UFO sightings, river monsters and other strange quirks of nature.

She left Stanley the security guard checking his squeaky ear piece, and entered the revolving entrance door that opens to the first floor of the FIC (Federal Intelligence Center), where she encountered Colonel Martin Swan.

She frowned.

Alexis Grumman and Martin Swan both worked out of an FIC manual that spelled out the department's conduct and procedure rules. How ever, Lt General Grumman and Colonel Martin Swan stood pages apart. While Alexis adhered to the letter of the law, Swan's *Invisible Six* Unit was at one point, dis-banned for conduct unbecoming to federal agents. Namely, feeding a live man to a live alligator. Eventually, Swan's unit was reinstated

UNDER THE BUS

after General James "Iron Horse" Taylor agreed to revise the manual with assistannce from several congressional, hearing members.

"So, how was your honeymoon, Martin?"

"My honeymoon was fine," said Swan giving the lieutenant general a smart salute.

"And the child bride?"

"Jodie is fine," said Swan dropping the salute, "And how's your boy toy?"

"Agent Jeremy Wade is fine and thank you for asking," replied Alexis in frozen tones.

Colonel Martin Swan and Alexis Grumman were both *generation gappers* which is a polite way of saying *cradle robbers*. Former Agent Wade was the same age as Skip Grumman, the son Alexis had out of wedlock years back, and Jodie Seales Santinio married Swan to gain a father for her four year old son, who is currently making a mark in the world, as firebug of the year. Thus far, the child prodigy has to his credit, one tool shed, one barn, two hay wagons, and is now back home in Tennessee, trying to set fire to Lake Norris.

"I understand there's a baby Jeremy," said the colonel.

"I gave birth to twin girls, Martin."

"Sorry," said Martin Swan, "Stanley must have gotten that wrong."

"Yes, Stanley does get things wrong."

The Department For Paranormal Activities now sits on the third floor of the F.I.C. building, due to second floor expansion of satellite imagery. The DPA offices are loaded with scanners, computers and wall screens that connect to a virtual net working system that interfaces with the FBI, CIA and numerous other federal departments. Alexis walked past the deserted receptionist desk and into the screening room, calling out, "You here, Doug?"

"I'm here."

"Where's JoJo?"

"Joanne left for her daily Covid19 test," replied the invisible projectionist, "I see you that bumped into the heralded Martin Swan, down stairs."

UNDER THE BUS

"Swan is a fraud," said Alexis dropping into one of a dozen, black leather swivel chairs, "I need you to drop the big wall screen."

"General, with all due respect, Martin Swan is not thought of as a fraud. Colonel Swan is recognized as a legend in his own time. Blowing up bridges in the face of the Taliban. Trading gunfire with Colombian drug lords."

"Sorry Doug, I didn't realize you were such a big Martin Swan fan," said Alexis staring at an empty glass pot, "I see JoJo made no coffee before she left."

"My favorite Martin Swan saga is the mid-flight abduction recovery," bubbled on the talkative but unseen projectionist who never saw a day of field duty, "The story goes that four terrorists kidnapped an ambassador's daughter in Frankfurt, Germany. They then commandeered an Arianna airliner and headed in the direction of Afghanistan. Sometime later when radio contact was reestablished, the plane landed safely at Kabul International Airport. The girl was now back in

Germany. The four terrorists were dead in the baggage compartment, with a note that read: *Compliments of Martin Swan and The Invisible Six."*

"Bravo," said Alexis, "Will you lower the giant wall screen?"

"And what about the plight of Pompeii?"

"As I recall," scoffed Alexis, "Terrorists wished to blow up the Pompeii ruins, yo ho."

"Yes, but innocent bystanders could have been injured," countered Doug, "Or maybe even killed."

It happened between 911 and the fall of Saddam Hussein. Headline seekers world 'round sought to blow up something – sometimes them selves. Airport security doubled. Scanners became a household word. Somehow twelve terrorists managed to obtain Swiss Guard uniforms and enter this early Roman city, buried under volcano ash in 79AD. At one point in history, Pompaii was lost for over 1500 years. Today, thanks to diligent excavation efforts, the Ruins are a tourist attraction

UNDER THE BUS

that consists of wounded walls and stone laid streets.

The terrorists synchronized watches. Clouds were dark, the air chilly. Mount Vesuvius loomed in the background. Each militant wore a wide dynamite belt beneath his orange and blue garb. They hid behind silent buildings and waited for tourists. None came. They decided to blow up the ruins with strategically placed car bombs.

Suddenly, the sky rained parachutes.

"Let me guess," said Alexis, "Martin Swan and The Invisible Six."

"You nailed it, first try."

"Doug, are the Invisible Six still monitoring Olan Chapman's cabin in Lake Powhattan, N.J."

"They better be," said the projectionist, "Chapman is still Number One on America's Most Wanted list."

"Lower the giant screen."

"Yes, ma'am."

The giant screen covered one entire wall of the viewing room. It didn't always lower properly, but it was helpful for reading tag numbers and other small details that might go unnoticed. It also provided a panoramic view of landscape areas. Alexis was interested in the surveillance tape of the Chapman residence on the day of the shooting, because the wide angle view of that clip would show Cabins 16, 18 and 20.

"Nothing suspicious happened at Cabin 18 on that particular day," said the projectionist as he fast-forwarded the tape, "No deliveries. . . no unusual vehicles . . . no Olan Chapman, . . no Henry Teasdale."

"We are not interested in Cabin 18," explained the lady general, "We are focused on Cabin 20, next door."

"We?"

"This is a request from Olan Chapman."

"Thee Olan Chapman?"

"Thee Olan Chapman."

"And just how does Olan Chapman hack his way into your personal communicator?"

"Doug, you are the geek, you tell me and we willl both know."

UNDER THE BUS

Chapman, Alexis and the Invisible Six formed a trio that dated back to Olan's first transformation into a forest ranger, named Jesse Joe Jacks. The saga ended when the Invisible Six chased Chapman over Niagara Falls, as Alexis watched helplessly from a headquarters monitor. Sometime later their paths crossed again when Olan morphed into an 18th Century artillery soldier who tried to shoot a nuclear armed missile out of the Mount Loyal N.J. Skyline.

"And he didn't miss by much," remembered the FIC projectionist.

"Doug, we need to be watching this film."

"Watching."

"And what do you see?"

"Nothing."

"I don't see anything, either," murmured the lady general, " Anyway, have this film footage sent to Hobbs Creek NJ, in care of Police Chief, Alvin Phillips."

"We can't wire it.?"

"Doug, I'm not sure Hobbs Creek even has

indoor plumbing."

"One more question," said the voice from behind the wall, "Why are we doing this for America's Most Wanted man?"

Alexis Grumman Wade paused to pop a candy mint between her oval lips. She took a sip of ice water and said, "This is not for Chapman. This is for his wife, who claims that Olan only fights for Truth, Justice and the American Way."

UNDER THE BUS

Chapter 26

Sgt Donde Clark raced between a double row of black and white squad cars, and screeched to a stop on the ground floor of the Hobbs Creek Police Station. The sudden jolt threw his mini partner into the windshield.

"Es theese more big news?" muttered Sgt Juanito Lewis wiggling free from a snagged seat belt, "Or are we just late for our donut."

"This is big!" said Donte closing out a call from dispatch, "This could wrap up the case."

The two men scampered up the rear steps of the station house and paused at the dispatch desk. Isabel Jackson still had her face down while she continued to pound on the glass overlay, smeared with coffee stains. The two men shrugged and burst into Chief Alvin Phillips' office.

"This is big," said township's top cop, "This is even bigger than Tom Dempsey's 63 yd field goal."

"Who's Tom Dempsey?" asked Donde.

"I theek he was some kind of prize fighter," said Juanito doing a cartwheel over the trash can."

Phillips already had Sgt Springer and the rolling projector set up to show this latest break through in the Richard Ghetti murder case. The film began at 7am on the morning of the shooting, and showed the front and only entrances to Cabins 16, 18 and 20. The film ended late that evening with the arrival of Detective Sergeants, Donde Clark and Juanito Lewis.

Alvin Phillips touched a match to a forbidden, black stogie, rocked back in the squeaky swivel chair, and blew a victorious smoke ring toward the overhead ceiling fan, saying "Do you see it.?"

"I see a bald spot beginning at the back of my head," lamented Juanito, now breathing heavy from a sitting position in front of the portable screen.

"Well, Ghetti left for work," said Donde, "I saw Ivy Chapman step outside twice, once to feed

UNDER THE BUS

the birds and once to feed the rabbits .. and, I saw Richard Ghetti return home from work."

"I didn't see Ms Ghetti's intruders," noted Juanito now focused on the screen.

"Sonofabitch, Chief," cried Donde, "Where are Ms Ghetti's intruders?"

"They are not there," confirmed Phillips, "No one entered that cabin on the day of the shooting, until Richard Ghetti came home from work."

"So, we got her!" cried Donde.

"We got her," said Hobbs Creek's top cop.

Alvin Phillips victorious smoke rings faded fast as he hung up from a call with the N.J. State Attorney's Office. He slammed down the phone and stomped to the window that served as his getaway perch when red tape began to smother wisdom. Car horns filled the parking lot air and he let the brown metal sash fall with a bang.

"What is it, Chief?" asked Donde.

"Gallegar wants the gun barrel."

"But, we don't need the gun barrel," pointed

out Donde, "We have enough evidence to make this case."

"According to Gallegar," said Phillips taking a long breath, "All we have is an overload of unsubstantiated poppycock. Gallegar says because of the magnitude of this case, and it's world wide attention, we're not going to trial without covering all bases."

"And the ballistic report that will link all three shootings, hinges with that gun barrel," chipped in Juanito Lewis.

"Exactly," replied Phillips. "So, you two are on your way back to Lake Powhattan. And you don't come back without that barrel."

"And just how do we do that, Chief?"

Phillips returned from his window perch and sat back down at his desk. He folded hands behind head and stared remorsefully at the ceiling fan as he said, "Well, where there's a will, there's a way. I'm sure two clever detectives from the Big Apple will come up with something."

Suddenly, Juanito Lewis finished some

UNDER THE BUS

pushups, jumped to his feet and stood at parade rest facing the varnished station house desk. "We do have a saying back in the Big Apple," said the midget, "It goes like this: *where there's a will, there's a relative.*"

Footnote: Tom Dempsey was a placekicker in the NFL who played for the N.O. Saints, Philadelphia Eagles, L.A. Rams, Houston Oilers, and Buffalo Bills. In 1970, while kicking for the Saints, Dempsey booted a 63 yd field goal that stood as a milepost for over 40 years.

Chapter 27

December 23, 2020

    St Thomas beaches truly have a magnetic draw that lies beyond species comprehension. These endless stretches of white sand attract game show winners, nine to five motorists looking to escape stop and go traffic, sun bathers wishing to change skin color from white to shiny brown. Occasionally, this U.S. owned territory becomes a hideaway for fugitives and deserting wives.

    Such was the case with Elizabeth Ghetti and Ivy Chapman Teasdale, two female residents from Hobbs Creek, NJ., who lay now basking in the afternoon sun, within eye reach of that magic point where ocean water touches blue heaven. Said the widow Ghetti in a smithy tone, "So, money can buy anything."

    Ivy Chapman rolled onto her tummy and stared across the rocky reefs at the orange roof

UNDER THE BUS

shingles that covered their hotel lodging. They chose this island site because no passport was needed – just a driver ID. And, in a world of choking security checkpoints, St Thomas was a breath of fresh air. Replied Ivy, "Hank has B.O."

"B.O.?"

"Body odor."

"Ivy, I know what body odor is and we all know my offer of five million dollars is why you are here, not body stink from a plumber who works with his head down a septic tank."

Two days back, Detective Sgts Donde Clark and Juanito Lewis laid out the straight skinny for the *Not So Merry Widow.* They told Elizabeth Ghetti that law enforcement held security tapes that proved there were no intruders who entered her cabin on the day that her husband was murdered. The revealing tape had filmed Richard Ghetti – and only Richard Ghetti – leaving and returning to Cabin Twenty. Elizabeth Ghetti's response to this information was typical Elizabeth Ghetti. She lit a cigarette and blew a small cloud of white smoke at the two law officers from New York City. Donde produced handcuffs. After which, the widow countered with the five million dollar bribe, which added up to 15 million: five for Donde; five for Juanito, and five for her secret confidant, Ivy Chapman Teasdale.

"Liz, they are not going to take the money."

"They will take the freaking money, Ivy. I know cops. Make the bribe big enough and the bastards will burn their ID card."

"Dam, you are bullheaded," cried Ivy sitting up in the sand to face Elizabeth, "Can't you see this is a trap. These two cops are conning you."

Elizabeth Ghetti took a few full body selfie's and then smacked her cell phone like a child's hand caught in a cookie jar. The tiny screen read *connection lost.* She cradled the device beneath her beach towel to remove glare and tried vainly again to reach her social network. "Dam carrier. I promised my followers a photo of me in my new bikini."

UNDER THE BUS

"They are looking for the barrel," said Ivy.

"They are looking for skin shots."

"Liz, the cops are looking for the barrel."

"What barrel?"

"Liz, everyone this side of the Mississippi knows you popped Richard."

"Richard needed to be popped," said the merry widow, "He had bad breath and he farted in bed. Do you know what it's like to sleep with a man who farts in bed?"

"Yes. .well.. now the cops want the steel tube that fits into the slide."

Elizabeth Ghetti stopped fiddling with her phone and turned full attention to her Hobbs Creek neighbor who was now tummy down, facing the ocean.

Continued Ivy, "The authorities know you used a calibration convertor that fits a forty-five. Hank found the magazine in your toilet trap and the midget found the slide under your kitchen sink. But, the barrel was missing and they need that missing sleeve to match scratches. They have some empty shells and if those casings match that barrel, you're in the big house and I'm out five million dollars."

"Ivy, it would be very stupid of me to ditch the slide and the magazine and keep the barrel," pointed out the widow, "They are here for the money."

"Liz, they are not here for the money!" insisted Ivy, "They are looking for the barrel. They are just waiting for an excuse to execute a search and seizure maneuver."

Elizabeth Ghetti opened her handbag and lit a cigarette. A giant boulder lay to her front. A sea grape tree flanked her shore side. A torn flag pole stood to her rear. As she studied the insignia, Detective Sgts, Donde Clark and Juanito Lewis shot up from the warm Carribean waters, gasping for air, arms waving, voices jubilant. Said the widow in flat tones, "I'll take Donde, you take the midget."

"Of course," replied Ivy, "You get the center-cut and I get the spoils."

Gentle horseplay and water splashing followed,

UNDER THE BUS

after which, Lewis and Clark with maidens in hand, took off to explore Sapphire Beach, St Thomas Island.

*   *   *   *   *

2am

Elizabeth Ghetti left the hotel in housecoat and sandals, with a flashlight in one hand and a white metal curtain rod in the other. The beach was quiet, as were the crickets. Also missing was moonlight. She flip-flopped along until she reached the giant sea grape tree. She looked around to see no one in sight. She lined up between the giant boulder and the torn beach marker, dropped to her knees and used the stolen, shade holder to etch a six foot circle in the sand.

A stubborn nightmare had ruined her sleep. Ivy's surveillance warning kept ringing through what should have been an easy, peaceful slumber. Instead, Elizabeth kept waking from a nightmare that clearly showed a metal tube protruding from washed away beach sand.

KYLE KEYES

She paused to light a cigarette and then began to dig. The damp sand caked beneath her nails and she cursed herself for not wearing gloves. She started at center circle and worked her way to the perimeter. At first, she uncovered nothing and panic began to set in. She dug faster and faster to the point of fury. Then, she felt the gun barrel that was now the sought after object. Relief filled her body. She pulled the metal sleeve from the sand and was just giving it a kiss when the first flashlight beam hit her in the face.

Two more flashlight beams followed, one from behind the giant boulder, and one from behind the innocent looking, sea grape tree.

"What do we have there, Ms Ghetti?" called out Donde Clark.

Elizabeth Ghetti froze momentarily when faced by the two detective sergeants and Ivy Teasdale. Then the widow jumped to her feet and hurled the gun barrel toward the ocean waters.

"Juan!" shouted Donde to his partner who was already underway.

UNDER THE BUS

Sometimes, justice requires exact timing. The midget and the missile reached ocean's edge at the same second, where Juanito caught the gun barrel before the metal sleeve hit the water. Said Donde examining the calibration convertor, "You should have disposed of this a long time back."

"She was using it as a brace to keep her handbag rigid," explained Ivy, "I saw her bury it here in the sand. She was pretending to light a cigarette while I was pretending to look the other way."

"You bitch !" screamed Elizabeth Ghetti, "You stupid, no good fucking bitch !"

"Elizabeth," purred Ivy, "Hank may have rotted teeth and smelly feet, but at least he's a warm body on a cold night, which is more than you're going to have where you are going."

"You bitch ! You no good fucking bitch !!!"

"Be advised Ms Ghetti," said Donde producing a pair of handcuffs, "Ivy Teasdale is a matron for the Hobbs Creek, Police Force. Chief Phillips swore her in before we left the mainland. Also, before I read you your rights, be advised that St Thomas Island is territory that belongs to the United States."

UNDER THE BUS

Chapter 28

December 25, 2020
Christmas time:

Light snow covered the earth in Hobbs Creek West, home of the two story farmhouse, rented by the Clarks, Donde and April Jean. Red and green bulbs out- lined the wrap-around porch. A Nativity scene, coupled with an array of cartoon cutouts spotted the front yard. Real candles glowed in the multiple pane windows, because April Jean loved the look and the fragrance that went with the holiday.

Inside, a four foot *Charlie Brown Christmas Tree* took center stage because neither Donde nor April Jean wanted to let go of this heirloom rooted in yesterday's memories. The Clarks married on a cheap beer budget, and found the tree at a Brooklyn garage sale. Somehow, as they moved up the social ladder, the tree followed. Now, it sat surrounded by gift wrapped packages, under a ceiling fan, facing a real log fireplace.

"Well, I would not have it in my home," said Juanito sliding down the banister that led to the second floor, "If I had a home."

"Oh you poor boy," lamented April Jean tying on an apron and pretending to play a violin, "Why don't you give us a rendition of the Boll Weevil Song, *Looking For A Home.*"

"I'm going for firewood," said Donde stepping out the back door.

Soon, the smell of ham and pineapple filtered into the front room, followed by April Jean's mellow voice, "Juan, can I see you here in the kitchen?"

"Yes, ma'am."

"That was pretty much a long shot that Elizabeth Ghetti would still be in possession of that gun barrel."

"Well, Columbus took a chance."

"And he came through St Thomas?"

"Supposedly."

UNDER THE BUS

"I've never been to St Thomas," murmured April Jean Clark, "What's it like?"

"It's one of the Virgin Islands," replied Juanito smelling a pot of spinach, "When you've seen one, you have seen 'em all as far as I'm concerned."

"And honeymooners go there?'

"They do." "

"The way I understand it," said April, "You were teamed up with Ivy Teasdale, and Donde accompanied Elizabeth Ghetti."

"Yes, ma'am."

April Jean stopped checking the oven temp and turned to face the midget, "Juan, I know you guys don't rat each other out. . but. .I have to know . . where did Donde have his Stutz Bearcat parked?"

Sergeant Lewis stopped executing back flips and faced the anxious woman. He grinned ever so slightly and emptied his side pockets.

Four paper receipts fell to the floor.

April Jean didn't understand at first, then she did understand. She scooped up the paper receipts. Each slip had a different number causing her to cry out, "You had separate rooms!"

"I made the sleeping arrangements," said the midget.

A joyous April threw the receipts upward, and swung Juanito in circles as Donde returned with an armload of wood.

"And what is this?" queried Sgt Donde Clark.

"It's your little buddy," bubbled April, "Juanito just gave me the best Christmas gift, ever."

… UNDER THE BUS

The End

KYLE KEYES

Plots and characters that form this storyline are fictional, as is the weather. Public Domain and fringe area details are true. All storyline names are fictional, and any resemblance to persons living or dead is purely coincidental.

There is no FIC (Federal Intelligence Center), and any descriptions or procedures described here-in, may or may not correspond with the whole, or any part of our national Intelligence Community (IC), which encompasses the FBI, CIA and various other intelligence agencies. There is no Eastern By Pass in Virginia, and any other topography features that interface with this storyline, are purely fictional.

There is no Lower Elk County in New Jersey, nor is there a Hobbs Creek, Carson City or Mount Loyal.

Product name usage is not an endorsement by author, publisher or printing house.

UNDER THE BUS

Public Domain information taken from the Philadelphia Inquirer, Camden Courier Post, Bradenton Herald and Online encyclopedia Wikipedia.

Topographic data supplied by Google Maps

Cover picture taken by author.

KYLE KEYES

UNDER THE BUS

All Rights Reserved

KYLE KEYES

Printed in Great Britain
by Amazon